FEMALE DISRUPTORS

FEMALE DISRUPTORS:

STORIES OF
MIGHTY FEMALE SCIENTISTS

MINDI MESSMER

NEW DEGREE PRESS

FEMALE DISRUPTORS:

Stories of Mighty Female Scientists

ISBN   979-8-88504-128-7 *Paperback*

        979-8-88504-758-6 *Kindle Ebook*

        979-8-88504-237-6 *Ebook*

This book is dedicated to my sons, Justin and Kegan, who make me proud every single day, and my husband, Mike, for his patience and support.

"As scientists, they were atypical women, as women, they were unusual scientists."

— MARGARET ROSSITER

CONTENTS

—

FOREWORD

———

The content and timing of this book are very relevant. In the past several years, and some would say longer, we have seen how science has been diminished by the politically motivated. We face critical public health threats relating to cancer and climate change; we have not yet accounted for the total future toll. As we look to the future, it is critical that all voices are heard and that everyone has an equal seat at the table. The content is relevant for young and old, male and female, and everyone who has a stake in our future.

On a more personal note, in my work in serving the public in the cancer prevention education space, I have had the great privilege of seeing extraordinary women paving the way toward protecting the health and saving lives of individuals, families, and communities. This book brings to light the critical and transformative leadership of women who have been defenders of human health and the environment. I find it ironic that while so many women in their life-saving work have fought to protect human health, they themselves face a wide breadth of disparities and inequities, including access to basic and gender-based health care.

I am incredibly grateful to Mindi, among other things, for her leadership in identifying the pediatric cancer clusters in New Hampshire, for her sharing her story, and for telling the stories of several women who have made the world a healthier place.

Thank you, Mindi.

Bill Couzens
Founder, Less Cancer

SOMETIMES IT'S A SPRING RAIN, SOMETIMES IT'S A TYPHOON

———

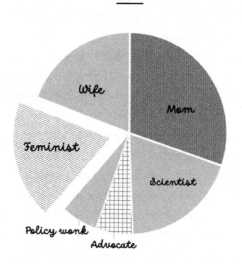

In early March 2020, we were standing in line in the Sint Maarten airport returning from the first vacation we had taken together in many years. To begin my re-entry into reality from the remote island of Saba, I looked at the newsfeed on my phone. The news about the spreading COVID-19 virus was concerning. I was a little worried that we would have issues with our flight home, but we did not.

The following week after we had returned, my husband didn't feel well. He also developed lesions on his back that we thought were a skin infection from scuba diving. On March 27, 2020, late at night, he called his doctor because he was having trouble breathing. They told him to go to the local emergency room, which was on lockdown. I thought he had COVID-19. It turned out to be leukemia, and he was rushed by ambulance to a hospital in Boston that night.

The Boston hospitals were all in lockdown. I immediately queried the nurses by phone about the protocols for protecting my husband from contracting COVID-19 while he fought the very acute attack from his cancer. Hospital administrators and staff were developing protocols on the fly, and the lack of personal protective gear for health care workers made them even more stressed. The hospital had separate elevators for doctors, nurses, and staff transportation to the oncology floor, where my husband spent most of his time in the hospital. The nurses told me they were self-isolated; they committed themselves to only spending time with their colleagues to protect the patients. No family members were allowed to enter the oncology ward. While it pained me not to be by his side, I knew that the strict no-visitor policy would be the best way to protect him from contracting COVID-19.

For the rest of us, across the United States, cities and towns were in lockdown as COVID-19 case numbers exploded. Beaches in my town were closed, and schools, colleges, universities, and restaurants shut down. The local tourist economy was shuttered. Zoom meetings had become the practiced norm for conducting business and academic meetings. Schools went to remote learning. News outlets reported tales of horrific illnesses and mounting deaths in European cities.

Ironically, since 2014, I have been fighting for state agencies to recognize and act on the high pediatric cancer rates in my community and state. I had been worried about my sons getting cancer because kids they went to school with were diagnosed with rare cancers. I worried about what was causing the children's cancers.; there might have been something in the environment triggering their cancer.

Starting in 2016, as a legislator, I've worked to create policy for cancer prevention; my husband's diagnosis became a horrible reality that brought my work directly to my front doorstep. I never expected my husband to be diagnosed with severe, rare, aggressive cancer. He was a healthy eater, worked out, and was young for that kind of diagnosis. The truth is, you can do everything within your power to prevent cancer, as my husband did, but it still might take you down. The pandemic added stress on top of the trauma of the cancer diagnosis, and I worried for my sons, who also had to face the fact that their father was seriously ill while dealing with life during a global lockdown.

The pandemic and cancer diagnosis came after a disappointing primary bid loss for an open congressional seat. It had been a family effort: everyone had pitched in, making signs, and going door to door to ask voters to vote for me. After I lost, I decided to run for the Executive Council, a unique elected executive branch body in New Hampshire. My older son worked on my campaign after finishing his senior year at Boston University, when he lived alone in Boston in a small apartment. After graduating from high school without fanfare, my younger son lived with me under lockdown—it was the scariest time for all of us. For me, having a campaign to run, albeit also remotely, during this time gave my son and me something productive to do when so many things were out of our control.

In late August 2020, when the primary election was a few weeks away, my mother wound up in the hospital again in upstate New York. Now, both my mother and husband were in hospitals under lockdown—what the hell was I going to do? It was yet another upsetting and unbelievable turn in the unending typhoon of my life.

My mother had been a registered nurse. Later in her career she was an organizer and then vice president of the nurses' union in New York City, fighting for the rights of nurses in the workplace. I have many memories of her tales, from the picket lines and labor negotiations. The labor disputes were always in part over wages but also respect for the nurses and their expertise. I remember visiting the picket line with her when the nurses were locked out of their jobs by the (ironically named) Sisters of Mercy, standing in the freezing cold just before Christmas. I was proud to be with her; the nurses treated her like a rock star. That Mercy strike resulted in the largest nurses' labor settlement in New York history.

"Anne was a leader and champion for nurses and the underdog. She was fearless and dedicated... Her leadership and battle with nurses resulted in so many of us [able to] retire with great pensions. Because of Anne, nurses gained parity with NYC nurses and greater respect for the way we were treated."

—SUE VAN ETTEN

My mother had been sick on and off for many years, having been diagnosed with breast cancer. Ironically, or maybe due to a higher force, I fought to reduce environmental exposures that can trigger breast cancer and leukemia.

Unfortunately, like so many others, my mother died in late August under lockdown in the hospital, and I could not be with her. While I knew she was sick, on some level, perhaps I was just so consumed with all of it that I didn't realize how ill she was; her death was another traumatic blow. Like me, at one time, she had entertained a political bid, so she would have been proud to see that I decidedly won the primary for the Executive Council about a week after her death.

Now, later in life, I realize I inherited my passion for fighting for my cause from my mother. But I had spent my life honing my scientific skills, becoming more adept at communicating science and data and facts, not feelings. I worked in a male-dominated engineering and scientific profession for most of my career. I was often one of a few women in academic and corporate settings. Around the same time that I began my career in science, a female scientist colleague applied for an agency job; she was the only woman hired. But before her boss decided on her hiring, she told me, he went around asking all the men in the office if their wives would mind him hiring a woman scientist.

We have progressed from that time, but have we made enough progress?

I had stepped into the political arena to address environmental concerns and bring science into policy decisions. I went from sitting behind a computer every day to participating in televised campaign forums and speaking to hundreds of people at a time. Since my work had required me to talk about data and facts with no emotion, I had to take drama lessons to learn a whole new way of delivering a message.

That was a big change for me.

As a legislator, I introduced policies to hold polluters accountable, protect drinking water and prevent cancer, and formed commissions to study how to prevent environmentally triggered cancers and chronic illnesses in New Hampshire. But I was targeted by lobbyists, other legislators, and state agency staff with gender-coded language meant to undermine my efforts. People criticized my hair, clothes, and make-up. The lobbyists called me "emotional" when presenting supportive data and science. My expertise, credibility, and motivations were questioned and attacked in the process. Finally, I noticed that my expertise seemed to be a detriment, while men I worked alongside were revered and respected for their expertise.

But as we look to the future, with the climate crisis upon us, we cannot afford to continue to sideline women and people of color, who are routinely discouraged from entering science fields and leadership positions or undermined when they do. Women are empathetic and passionate advocates for their families and communities. We bring diverse perspectives and approaches to problem-solving. Women must be heard, acknowledged, valued, and recognized for their contributions.

Unfortunately, decades of inaction and malfeasance have put us in the position we are in—the climate crisis and threats to our water, public health, environment, and wildlife. We cannot expect someone else to take care of it. We need all-hands-on-deck. We need scientists of varied backgrounds to address and solve complex issues like climate change, emerging from the pandemic, and preparing for the next pandemic. Climate change is an existential threat, and we have a moral obligation to future generations to create a paradigm shift to bring more people into the fold to find solutions. Every hurricane, tornado, or forest fire multiplies the threats caused by climate change.

As a mom, wife, scientist, advocate, former legislator, and feminist, my experiences provide a unique perspective. But now it's time to use that feminist slice of the pie. While interviewing other women scientists, I learned that their experiences were mine. As a female scientist with a diverse academic and professional background, I felt obligated to share my story and the stories of other female scientists, especially those who have laid the groundwork for the rest of us. But, while researching studies about gender bias in science, I discovered our stories were, unfortunately, more the norm than the exception.

In truth, writing this book has been challenging but cathartic for me as the pandemic drags into its third year. Science and women are under attack, and the impacts of agencies that have failed to protect us play out in my home, community, state, and nation. The pandemic created a perfect opportunity to connect with amazing women across the country because while we were isolated, Zoom meetings afforded new connections. Their stories are in this book.

It was challenging to bring these stories and my perspectives, which are sometimes not pleasant, in a not overly negative manner. But as a scientist, I'm not one to formulate flowery stories of false hope either.

I hope this book will empower women, help normalize female scientists in leadership positions, and encourage young women to enter science fields, use their voices, and inspire others to step up. I hope that men, young and old alike, will recognize and modify behaviors, conscious or unconscious, that undermine female scientists.[1]

---

1   Throughout this book, female scientists are women in science, technology, engineering, or mathematics fields.

PART 1

WHERE IT ALL STARTED

CHAPTER 1

SOUNDING THE ALARM

—

*"If you are on the right track, if you have this inner
knowledge, then nobody can turn you off...
no matter what they say."*

—DR. BARBARA MCCLINTOCK, 1983 NOBEL PRIZE
WINNER, PHYSIOLOGY OR MEDICINE

In January 2014, a boy who lived in my town and went to my
son's school was diagnosed with acute lymphocytic leukemia
(ALL).

In February 2014, another boy was diagnosed with rhabdomyosarcoma (RMS) cancer. He was twelve years old. I
knew the boy's mother; she was my aerobics and yoga teacher
for years. His mother noted, "He had been having a lot of
pain in his jaw, and it got progressively worse to the point
where it was visible and affecting his speech. It's something
you can't even imagine unless you're in it. It's terrifying; it's

just horrific to watch your kid go through something like that" (McMenemy, 2016a).

At the same time, my friend told me about two other children diagnosed with pleuropulmonary blastoma (PPB), another rare form of soft tissue sarcoma (Long, 2016).

A year earlier, Lydia Valdez, age nine, had died from RMS. Lydia had lived in the neighboring city of Portsmouth (Cook, 2013). A few years before that, Ellie Shoal Potvin died at age eight in June 2010. She was diagnosed with stage 4 RMS in July 2008. Her mother said Ellie died after enduring a "terrible chemotherapy regimen" (McMenemy, 2016).

RMS is exceedingly rare; only about 350 RMS cases are identified yearly in the United States (PDQ Pediatric Treatment Editorial Board, 2021). However, RMS is a devastating diagnosis because the prognosis for survival is poor. The survival rate for children with RMS is about 61 percent but much worse for adults (27 percent) (Hettmer et al., 2014). Genetic factors may contribute to RMS and PPB (PDQ Pediatric Treatment Editorial Board, 2021). But some environmental factors, including tobacco use and chemical exposure, are also thought to contribute to RMS and PPB risk (Grufferman et al., 1982; Zhang et al., 2019). In addition, environmental exposures like radiation, pesticides, or benzene are thought to trigger ALL (American Cancer Society, 2022; Ding et al., 2012).

I was concerned there were too many kids with environmentally triggered cancers in my town. By early 2014, I had taken several classes that covered topics like cancer clusters, epidemiology, and statistics as part of a master's degree program at Georgetown University in clinical science. Those classes provided me with a background in cancer clusters and statistical assessment of data on cancer and illness. I calculated the rate of kids with rare cancer in my town; it was about 542 times the national rate. I was shocked. I didn't believe my math and did the calculation several times.

Based on my calculations, it *did not seem* that the children's cancers were rare in my community.

To do the calculations, I used the number of kids I knew about; what if there were more children with cancer? I knew parents were devastated when they found out their child had cancer. As a mom of two who attended school in town, I also worried about my family. Specifically, my younger son still attended the same school as the kids with cancer. The cancers made me question whether there was an identifiable cause, whether the air or water was contaminated in the school or near their homes and had caused the kids to get sick. As an environmental scientist, I thought if something in the environment caused the cancers, someone should know to prevent it from affecting other children.

The Centers for Disease Control and Prevention (CDC)'s website instructs you to report your concerns to the state cancer registry or state agency. I searched the Internet and found that New Hampshire had a cancer registry. On March 3, 2014, I called Dr. Monawar Hosain, the state cancer epidemiologist, and told him about my concerns about the children with cancer in my town. A few days later, on March 6, 2014, I followed up with an e-mail to Dr. Hosain, detailing my concerns that the children's cancers, while rare, seemed not to be rare in my town.

PRODDING AND CAJOLING

Over the next two years, I e-mailed Dr. Hosain every so often to see if they had an answer yet. I also wanted to make sure they didn't think I would give up. Dr. Hosain said they were working on it each time I e-mailed or called.

As time went on, some of my friends and their friends continued to worry. Some knew I was an environmental scientist, and they asked my opinion. They asked me:

- "Isn't it odd that several kids in our town are diagnosed with the same types of rare cancer?"
- "Could there be an environmental issue like contaminated drinking water?"
- "Should I let my kids drink the water?"
- "Could emissions from the nearby Seabrook Nuclear Power Plant be causing the cancers?"
- "Is there something wrong in the elementary school?"

I did not have any definite answers for them. I had some of the same questions. Then, in August 2014, Sam Thomas died at age fourteen after being diagnosed with RMS (Foster's Daily Democrat, 2014). He lived in the neighboring town of North Hampton.

Meanwhile, the local press covered the Air Force's announcement in 2014 that they polluted the water supply at the former Pease Air Force base in Portsmouth. The city shut down the well when it found "forever chemicals," or per- and polyfluoroalkyl substances (PFAS), at unsafe levels (Leigh, 2021). The chemicals originated from firefighting and fire training activities on the former base. The city acquired the base and the water supply through the Base Realignment and Closure (BRAC) process in the mid-1990s (Leigh, 2021). Portsmouth water engineers also admitted the well had boosted the rest of the city's water supply, as needed.

PFAS are a group of more than twelve thousand chemicals (U.S. Environmental Protection Agency, 2021) used in products, including Teflon pans, waterproof rain gear, food packaging, firefighting aqueous film-forming foams (AFFF), plastics, dental floss, and many other consumer and medical products (Sunderland et al., 2019). PFAS are used in thousands of consumer products worldwide. PFAS or "forever chemicals" do not break down in the environment or your body. Instead, they accumulate in animals, fish, and humans. So far, we cannot remove the PFAS from our bodies, so it is imperative to prevent exposure. As a result, more than 90 percent of the world, including almost every baby born, have detectable levels of PFAS in their bodies at birth (Bilott, 2020).

I had first heard of "forever chemicals" in 2012 when I was managing a multisite environmental investigation at a Navy base in Maine. At a former fire training area, we found chemicals I had never heard of; but the Navy specialists seemed to know enough to direct me to sample for them as part of the investigation. The Navy also directed me to find the source of the groundwater contamination, which turned out to be about fifty buried 55-gallon drums at the edge of the fire training area. A white foamy substance leaked from punctured drums that spread across a small pond. A young woman on my field team got sick and went to the hospital from exposure. The Navy did not tell me what the substance in the drums was, but now I know they have known about the toxicity of AFFF since at least the 1980s (Environmental Working Group, 2018). However, it wasn't until 2020, more than eight years later, the Navy tested fifty-four private wells surrounding the fire training area, finding PFAS chemicals higher than the EPA's guideline (which is too high) in at least thirteen wells. As a result, the Navy provided families with bottled water when PFAS in their wells exceeded the EPA guideline (Alley, 2020).

Exposure to PFAS is linked to kidney and testicular cancer, congenital disabilities, liver disease, thyroid disease, decreased immunity, hormone disruption, and other serious health problems (C8 Science Panel, 2020). In addition, a growing body of scientific evidence shows a connection between PFAS exposure and immune system disruptions, reduced childhood vaccination efficacy, more severe COVID-19 outcomes, and cancers (Grandjean, et al., 2012; Grandjean, et al., 2020; Messmer et al., 2022).

After the public realized what had happened in Portsmouth, advocacy groups and elected officials pushed for blood testing for the workers and children at the day cares at the former base. The results showed that at least three thousand people, including 350 children, had elevated "forever chemical" levels in their blood, mostly due to drinking contaminated water. So, there was already a heightened public awareness and concern about drinking water safety in the community. Parents across the seacoast were concerned about their children who had attended the day care facilities at the former base.

The Air Force also admitted to using a long list of other chemicals at the base. Could some of these also have entered the Portsmouth water system with unknown results?

In late 2015, I was frustrated that I still didn't have an answer from Dr. Hosain. While talking to my friend, she suggested I reach out to my state representative to see if he could help shake out the answer. So, I e-mailed my state representative to solicit his help.

Finally, in early February of 2016, after two years of prodding, the state health department invited another mom and me to our town library for a meeting. Unfortunately, the state agency representatives would not share any details regarding their findings before we met.

**THE AGENCY OFFICIALS CONFIRMED MY SUSPICIONS.
THERE WAS A DOUBLE CANCER CLUSTER.**

On the evening of February 11, 2016, I walked into the library conference room and sat down. Another mom from my town was in the room, and four men (my state representative at the time, two state scientists, and a public relations person from the state health department). In addition, a woman from the state cancer registry from Dartmouth was on speakerphone.

The agency told us that the cancer rates checked all the boxes to qualify as a CDC-defined double cancer cluster (New Hampshire Department of Health and Human Services, 2016). The number of children diagnosed with two rare cancers (RMS and PPB) was higher than it should be in my town.

To be considered a cancer cluster, the cancers must meet the definition established by the CDC (Centers for Disease Control and Prevention, 2019). The CDC definition specifies that the cancers occur over a specific time interval, within a selected geographic area, within a particular population, with known common causation (Centers for Disease Control and Prevention, 2019). While the CDC strictly defines the constraints for cluster cancers, agencies have the latitude to adjust one or more parameters of the definition. The state agency selects the time frame and the geographic location and assesses whether the cancers have a common cause during a cancer cluster assessment. For example, the agency can reduce the cancers included in the analysis by restricting the time frame or geographic area. In addition, the CDC specifies that "cases must involve the same type of cancer, or types of cancer scientifically proven to have the same cause" (Centers for Disease Control and Prevention, 2019).

Most of the time, when a member of the public reports what they perceive to be a cancer cluster, that agency does not conclude that the cancers meet the definition of a CDC-defined cancer cluster. Cancer cluster determinations are exceedingly rare (National Cancer Institute, 2018). For example, a 2021 study determined that over the preceding twenty years, only seventy-two of the 576 reported cancer cluster investigations conducted met a cancer cluster definition. Only three of the seventy-two cancer clusters were linked to environmental exposures (asbestos, contaminated drinking water, industrial air, and water pollution).[2] Only one cancer cluster was linked to a clear cause (Goodman et al., 2012).

The agency report on the cancer clusters "did not find any scientific evidence that development of RMS is linked to environmental or behavioral risk factors" (New Hampshire Department of Health and Human Services, 2016). According to the report, the agency eliminated potential environmental exposures from Seabrook Nuclear Power Plant and the Schiller Station (coal) as possible cancer causes but gave no information on how they conducted the evaluation. The report also dismissed the drinking water contamination at Pease Air Force Base in the neighboring town of Portsmouth as a possible factor in causing the cancers.

---

2   An example of a cancer cluster was detailed in the movie *A Civil Action*. The film told the story of a childhood leukemia cluster in Woburn, MA. The public water supply on Woburn was contaminated by W.R. Grace and possibly linked to the cancer cluster (Zaillian et al., 1998). In May 1979, barrels of industrial fluid containing trichloroethylene (TCE) and perchloroethylene (PCE) had been leaking into the Aberjona River (Domagalski, 1999). The state conducted a cancer cluster investigation in response to public concerns and identified an increased incidence of leukemia in boys but not girls (Cutler et al., 1986). But, forty-three years later, the Superfund site still isn't cleaned up (U.S. Environmental Protection Agency, 2022).

The agency definition for the cancer cluster included RMS and PPB cancer cases between 2005 and 2014. Were earlier cancer rates higher before 2005 also? Was there a recent environmental issue potentially contributing to the cancers, or was it something older? The more I looked, the more I was convinced the latter was true. An environmental advocate shared two pieces of information with me. One document was a state-issued brief dated January 2009. The first report detailed that childhood cancer rates in New Hampshire between 1990 and 2005 were high compared to US national rates (New Hampshire Division of Health and Human Services, 2009). The same cancers, RMS and PPB, were on the list that included nineteen other RMS cancers and 238 cases of soft tissue sarcomas total between 1990 and 2005 (Office of Health Statistics and Data Management, 2009). All the most common cancers, including soft tissue sarcomas, are thought to be, at least in part, environmentally triggered. The second report indicated that childhood cancer mortality in my county increased 49.2 percent for ages up to nine years old between 1990 and 2014 compared to 1973 through 1989, while the childhood cancer mortality decreased in the rest of New Hampshire.

CALL FOR ACTION

At the library meeting, I pushed the state to investigate potential factors causing the kids' cancers. I knew an investigation to determine the cancers' possible causes would be complicated and arduous, and there was no time to waste. As a lifelong scientist, I routinely used data to decide how and when to act. It seemed that they hadn't tried very hard to look for potential causes for the cancers.

But the men in the room asserted it might be a statistical fluke; they wanted to wait and see if more cancers cropped up. Waiting to see if more kids got sick when the agency admitted the cancers were a concern made no sense. If the state agencies could determine the problem causing the cancers, or at least look, they could act before more kids got sick.

For example, I suggested they could sample the water supply. Or perhaps, I said, the state environmental services could collect soil samples from the school playground or their yards at home. I suggested they could collect blood samples to find any common threads between the children. The agency denied every suggestion I made to investigate the issue with flimsy excuses. Moreover, with every offer of advice, the public relations person, Jake Leon, seemed to become more exasperated with me.

They replied, "What would we test for?"

Their inaction was a threat to my community. It concerned me that the agency wanted to dismiss the cancer cluster without collecting any data. How could the agencies tasked with public health protection not even try to investigate possible causes of the children's cancers? In addition, based on what I heard, there was no clear path to trigger action.

So, I asked the men in the room, "What would make you all take action?"

No one in the library conference room had an answer. Silence.

I left the meeting at the library with a mixture of emotions: anger, shock, frustration, and worry. I was flabbergasted. Over the next few days, I unpacked what had happened.

**WHEN I LEFT THE LIBRARY, IT SEEMED CLEAR
THAT NO ONE ELSE IN THAT MEETING WOULD ACT.**
Their do-nothing approach did not sit well with me. Innocent children had died and were dying. Didn't the agency
see the GoFundMe drives to support the families?

On February 23, 2016, I received another e-mail from
Dr. Hosain that thanked us for our concerns, stated that it
was "unfortunate," and it was important for them to "hear
about cancer-related concerns from the community and
address them as best we can." However, hearing about the
concerns, acknowledging an issue, and dropping the ball
wasn't enough for me. From the e-mail, it seemed that the
agency was firmly closing the book on the cancer cluster
issue without any intention of further action.

On February 24th, eleven days after the library meeting, I drove to Logan Airport in Boston to catch a flight to
Washington, DC, to attend a meeting at Georgetown University. On the way, I went through the backstreets of East
Boston to avoid traffic, past the towering gas storage tanks.
I thought about how the residents of East Boston, nestled
around and among the gas storage tanks, could be getting
sick from environmental exposure. I also thought about
the library meeting, the cancer cluster designation, and the
e-mail I received the day before from Dr. Hosain. I knew
I would not be able to live with myself if one more child
was diagnosed with cancer and I hadn't done something to
push for action. But I was still working as an environmental
consultant, so I had to be careful. If my clients or industry
colleagues found out that I raised the issue publicly, I could
lose clients.

I thought about Jeff McMenemy, a local reporter, who
had done an excellent job chronicling the complicated Pease

water contamination issue discussed earlier in this chapter. His stories on the topic seemed to be well-researched and fair but communicated the threat in an evenhanded way. I decided to call him from my car before I got to the airport without giving him my name to see if he would report on the cancer cluster. I told him where to find the state's report on the cancer cluster determination buried on their website. He seemed very interested in the problem and said he would check it out. A few days later, on February 28th, I saw Jeff's first story on the cancer cluster designation in one of the seacoast newspapers (McMenemy, 2016d). The story was good. But the article quoted three men with an "MD" after their names, and each one minimized the issue. For example, one said, "It's hard to believe the cases were due to an environmental exposure" and "there are such small numbers" (McMenemy, 2016). As I read them, I second-guessed my actions.

But as the news spread, it became clear that most parents didn't buy it either. Parents, including the parents of children in the cancer cluster, had been unaware of an investigation until they read about it in the newspapers. The state epidemiologist admitted, "The state could have done a better job of letting parents know" (Hunter, 2016). The parents of the children with cancer pressed for action and investigation into potential causes of the cancers.

FACING THE MUSIC

In response to the push from parents, on March 15, 2016, the state health agency held a public meeting in our town. Residents expressed their anger and fear (Sexton, 2016).

"What you're dealing with in this community of residents in this five-town area is probably fear and anger and the sense of betrayal because there was no transparency."

—JILLIAN LANE, MOM AND ACTIVIST (TRIMBLE, 2016).

As I had feared, conversations led me to think that the state investigation may not have captured all the children with cancer. People began recounting other kids with cancers who may not have been counted because they had moved away.

"It took my wife and I about fifteen minutes to come up with seven, if not eight names."

—SAM THOMAS'S FATHER.
SAM DIED AT THE AGE OF FOURTEEN (SEXTON, 2016).

A mother of one of the children with RMS called the state's conclusions,

"ridiculous and absurd."

—MIMI CARPENTER (MCMENEMY, 2016).

For the parents whose children had cancer, I could only imagine their grief, their fears. I feared for my children and family because there might have been an unrecognized environmental threat in our town.

WHAT IF I WERE WRONG?

As I sat in the public meeting, I felt a sinking feeling and a sense of guilt for exposing the issue; I didn't want to cause the families any more pain or anguish. I did not want to be correct. It had taken two years, but the state confirmed my observations that the high rates of children with cancer in my community were unusual. The parents were angry that they hadn't been told before the media story was printed. By now, it seemed that they realized the agency's intention was not to act. Their anger made me feel that I had done the right thing. The parents of the children with cancer didn't think I was wrong. Parents did not buy the state's conclusion that environmental exposures didn't cause the cancers. They raised several issues that could be contributing to the children's cancers, including radiation emissions from nearby Seabrook Nuclear Power Plant or the Portsmouth Naval Shipyard or chemical exposures. The parents pressed elected officials for action.

The governor responded by creating the Seacoast Pediatric Cancer Task Force to investigate potential cancer-related environmental triggers. She appointed me to serve on that task force, and we got to work in June 2016.

The task force was under an intense media spotlight from the outset. We held our first meeting in a small room in a community center. National and state media recorded the session; spectators and the press overflowed into the hallway. But as a lifelong scientist, I found the media presence and the tensions between the agency and advocates on the task force unsettling. On the one hand, I was relieved to see so much media attention at the meeting that created a record of the event and increased awareness. But, on the other hand, it was upsetting to see the agencies push back on entirely logical next steps. During the first task force meeting, while the cameras were running, I pressed the state health department representative again to test the kids with cancer for chemicals. But, again, the state responded with excuses:

- What tests would they run on the samples?
- What would we do with that information?
- There is no precedence for what to do with blood test results of this nature with children.

The excuses rang hollow to me. As a parent and a scientist, I simply wanted to know if chemicals contributed to the cancers. But the state health agency representative tried to say it would be unsympathetic to the families by asking for blood testing, even though blood draws are common for people with cancer. I felt that I would comply to save others from the same tragedy if it were my child. The state agency had no intention of asking the parents. I could not understand why the agency decided to throw its hands up in defeat before even trying and deprive the community of answers.

When we moved to Rye, I thought we had escaped issues like this in Portsmouth that could be making people sick. I was relieved that the governor formed the task force; it seemed like an excellent place to get to the bottom of the issues. Even though my professional responsibilities might get messy, I knew I had to try to push for action.

CHAPTER 2

TOXIC SOUP

———

*"If you think you are too small to make a difference,
try sleeping in a closed room with a mosquito."*

—AFRICAN PROVERB

When my oldest son was born, we were living in Portsmouth. As a newborn, he seemed sick all the time. His little body was so covered with hives when I brought him to the pediatrician for vaccination when he was four months old that the nurse asked the doctor to come in and confirm it was okay to give him the shot. I was so tired from the two-hour breastfeeding twenty-four hours a day that I didn't realize the food I was eating might be triggering his immune system to react to typically innocuous foods I was eating. Then when he was about six months old, his allergic reactions were so severe and frequent that we took him to a doctor in Boston. He was diagnosed with multiple, severe, life-threatening allergies by a specialist at Children's Hospital in Boston. The doctor told me she had never seen a child with so many severe food allergies.

In kindergarten and elementary school, we had significant challenges with the school district. Eventually, the district placed him in a school in a neighboring town with only about forty students.

By the time he was in middle school, my son had been hospitalized eleven times for near-death reactions to eating food that had minute quantities of milk or peanuts or eggs.

I had suspected some environmental issues like the tap water could be the culprit for his unusual severe multiple allergies. Now I know my exposure to per- and polyfluoroalkyl substances (PFAS) chemicals could have caused my son's immune system to be triggered by normally innocuous food protein (Yu, Freeland, and Nadeau, 2016).

When my younger son entered fourth grade, we sold our house and moved to Rye. I thought it would be safer for my family and we had escaped my worries about contaminated drinking water.

TAKING ON THE TASK

Because so many had attended the first Seacoast Pediatric Cancer Task Force meeting in June 2016, we held the monthly meetings in the Portsmouth City Hall conference room. The room was much larger, and the city produced the recordings on local TV.

After brainstorming about possibilities we each knew, the task force began to map out a plan to examine possible environmental triggers for the cancers. For example, a community member raised concerns about the old Coakley dump at the edge of Rye (United States Environmental Protection Agency, 1983). Although the state report listed several potential environmental hazards, the Coakley Superfund dump, located geographically central to the cancer cluster, was not mentioned (New Hampshire Department of Health and Human Services, 2016). I wondered why the dump was omitted from the state's report. I vaguely remembered hearing about the dump through my environmental work, but it was so old I had always assumed it wasn't an issue anymore.

The task force members started to ask questions about the dump.

- Why didn't the state mention the dump as a possible environmental issue?
- How was the dump closed?
- What environmental work happened, and what was ongoing?
- What chemicals could be leaching out of the dump?
- Could the dump still pose an environmental threat to private and public water supplies?
- The Air Force used the dump too. Were "forever chemicals" or PFAS also put in the dump?

The task force pushed the regulators to require the polluter group to analyze groundwater samples for PFAS; they did.

DIGGING IN

The task force voted to form a subcommittee to focus on the dump so the commission could investigate other environmental hazards. I was appointed to chair the subcommittee. I naively expected everyone to roll up their sleeves and help us unearth the facts around this toxic dump that could be contributing to the children getting sick and dying from cancers.

At subcommittee meetings, some residents questioned the development of residential areas with private wells and irrigation systems that acted like straws drawing the chemicals out from under the capped landfill. Jillian Lane, a prominent advocate and resident in one of the developments, said, "I had zero idea, there was no disclosure [...]. There are definitely people who knew Coakley Landfill existed [...] but I don't think they knew exactly what kind of animal it was" (McMenemy, 2016a). More residents living within a mile of the dump shared their concerns about the safety of the water from their private wells that provided water for drinking, cooking, and bathing.

One of the fathers of one of the kids with RMS shared how, when he was young, he rode his bike through puddles of colored liquids around the dump with other kids. Historical agency reports also documented those colored puddles of chemicals, called breakouts, were observed around the dump by agency scientists in 1983 (United States Environmental Protection Agency, 1983).

I soon learned to expect the unexpected at the subcommittee meetings. I was shocked that some wanted to disrupt the meetings and shut down the discussion. Some feared their property values would decrease or that they would never be able to sell their homes. Tensions and frustrations peaked at one of them in November 2016 when a man interrupted me and stood up to speak.

He was agitated.

Mr. Ron Demo told us about his son, Steven, who died at forty-two from RMS, the same cancer that made up the cancer cluster in my community. Steven grew up in a house near the dump, and Mr. Demo described his son's interest in archaeology when growing up. Steven would grab a shovel and go down and dig along the train tracks every day after school. "That put him within a couple of hundred feet of the landfill," Mr. Demo noted (McMenemy, 2016b). Mr. Demo was frustrated because his son's death was neither counted nor recognized in the cancer cluster. I held back the tears when I heard Mr. Demo's story about his son in front of a room full of people in the basement of the public library, just one floor below where the state officials first denied my suggestions.

In response, the subcommittee pushed the state to provide Mr. Demo with a cancer cluster questionnaire sent to the other families so that his son's death could be acknowledged and counted.

Later that month, the subcommittee pushed for a public tour of the toxic dump. The regulators arranged the trip to be led by the paid consultant for the polluter group, Mike Deyling. Members of the subcommittee, the commission, regulators, public officials, and interested citizens attended. Mike Deyling finished the tour by saying, "If you can't see the houses from here where the kids died from cancer, the landfill didn't cause them." I was shocked by his lack of knowledge and callousness. I also knew he was entirely unqualified to make that kind of statement. Not only *could one see* from that vantage the house of Ron Demo and his son Steven, but one could also see where Steven would play archaeologist after school and dig up the ground in and near the dump.

RUNAWAY POLLUTION

As an environmental consultant, I sat in my kitchen and opened the 356-page report that included results for twenty-four groundwater samples collected from the toxic Coakley dump located at the edge of my town. My client worked for the Coakley Landfill Group (CLG), the group of businesses and municipalities that were deemed responsible for the pollution, which had been set up through a Consent Decree with the EPA in the early 1990s (Schreiber, 2010; United States Environmental Protection Agency—Region, I, 1991).[3]

As a consultant, my task was to sift through the massive document, examine how well the lab ran the tests, assess the accuracy of the results, and report how reliable the results were in estimating the level of chemicals in the samples. I relied on decades of experience and training to assess the laboratory results. The report showed exceptionally high concentrations of "forever chemicals" or PFAS in the samples, up to sixteen times the EPA health advisory. The chemicals were fifty times higher than most scientists and I would have preferred them at the time. My client contracted with me to do the work, so I could not speak about the chemicals in the water at Coakley until the state agency made the results public.

---

3   In 1991, the Participation Agreement that formed the responsible party group (Coakley Landfill Group [CLG]) allocated combined municipal responsibility at 63 percent (53 percent was assigned to the City of Portsmouth), 20 percent assigned to hazardous waste generators, and ~17 percent assigned to hazardous waste haulers (Consent Decree in the matter of *United States v. City of Portsmouth, NH, et al.*, September 27, 1991). The CLG holds 80 percent of the original responsibility for the cleanup since the Department of Defense had paid its 20 percent share of the responsibility in 1998 (https://www.govinfo.gov/app/details/FR-1998-11-19/98-30970). The 1998 Consent Decree resolved claims on behalf of the US Environmental Protection Agency against twenty-eight municipal, corporate, and other defendants.

But I sensed that my two worlds were colliding: the paid consultant that looks at data for polluters and the advocate who fought for the health of my community. Sooner or later, I knew I would have to address the conflict.

As an advocate, the questions I had about the Coakley dump led to some answers but more questions. The historical facts were confusing, made more complicated by complex technical issues. We also had to learn about a new "emerging" set of chemicals found in the dump. One of the most disturbing facts that began to emerge was that the manufacturers, the Department of Defense, and the EPA had known about the dangers of PFAS chemicals for decades, notably for pregnant mothers and their babies (Karrh, 1981).

HISTORY OF DENIALISM

As I studied the history of the dump, I realized that our concerns in 2016 were like those expressed decades before. Not much had changed since 1988. The old news stories that I read alarmed me. All that was different in the new ones were the dates and people's names.

A transcript from an EPA public meeting held in 1990 included Ms. Lilian Wylie's testimony. Ms. Wylie said she and Ms. Ruth Martin "were known as the two crazy ladies of Lafayette Terrace, screaming for nothing" (United States Environmental Protection Agency, 1990). They had begun raising concerns as early as 1975 (Russell, Lewis, and Keating, 1992).

"The water was so bad that you smelled worse after you took a shower," John Wylie told a reporter. "Everyone in the neighborhood stunk, but they didn't realize it. They were so used to it," Ms. Martin noted (Russell, Lewis, and Keating, 1992).

Finally, the state realized Ms. Martin's concerns were well-founded when her daughter was diagnosed with a kidney infection. Although the state initially denied her request to test her well water, in 1983, they tested her water only for bacteria and found none (Russell, Lewis, and Keating, 1992). Later in 1983, after Ms. Martin pressed again, the state finally retested her well and found high levels of five carcinogens in her water (United States Environmental Protection Agency 1990b). "They let us drink this water for ten years before they admitted anything was in there. It's scary because what we've gone through for the last ten years is [to be] stuck here with no help," noted a woman who raised a family on Lafayette Terrace during those ten years (Russell, Lewis, and Keating, 1992).

Shockingly, North Hampton officials accused Lafayette residents of polluting their own wells. Ultimately, the town extended public waterlines to the neighborhood (Russell, Lewis, and Keating, 1992).

INVISIBLE HEALTH CRISIS

Lafayette Terrace residents hoped that health studies they had pushed for would recognize and provide answers regarding illnesses in their neighborhood. However, in 1988, their hopes were dashed when the state and federal agencies separately concluded that there were no extraordinary health problems in the area (Agency for Toxic Substances and Disease Registry, 1988; New Hampshire Division of Public Health Services, 1988).

Ms. Wylie called the studies a "fraud, cover-up and a disgrace" (Young, 1988). Ms. Martha Bailey, a member of the National Toxics Campaign Fund, said, "I think the federal government is covering up. This area, southern Rockingham County, has the highest cancer rate in the state. But nobody is looking into why" (Young, 1988).

After releasing the 1988 health study report, Eugene Schwartz, the state epidemiologist, resigned, asserting that the governor suppressed the cancer study results that had found public health issues (Young, 1988). Schwartz filed a complaint, followed by an appeal, with the state labor board alleging he had been "harassed and retaliated against because he had been outspoken in his concern for the health and safety of New Hampshire citizens." Schwartz had left the agency to work for the Centers for Disease Control and Prevention (CDC) (New Hampshire Division of Public Health Services, 1989). In 1992, a supplement to the health assessment again concluded there were no significant health concerns for Lafayette Terrace residents (Agency for Toxic Substances and Disease Control, 1992).

The Lafayette Terrace residents' health concerns were justified, but their efforts faded with time.

"I was naive at first. If anything went wrong, I thought the state would take care of us."

—MS. LILIAN WYLIE,
LAFAYETTE TERRACE RESIDENT (YOUNG, 1988)

WHAT HAPPENED?
Inconclusive studies and inadequate action resulted in a multilayered failure of regulatory bodies that are supposed to function to protect public health. Money likely had a great deal to do with what happened. The original remedial estimate for the Coakley dump was over $20M; the Department of Defense chipped in $5M and stipulated the money would have to be refunded if the groundwater treatment system was

not installed (McMenemy, 2018). The CLG took the $5M from the Department of Defense but never installed the groundwater treatment system. The CLG, which is 63 percent funded by the taxpayers, will have to pay the $5M back at some point. Therefore, the taxpayers were left holding 63 percent of the $5M future liability. By 2019, the CLG had reportedly spent $17M but never installed a system to stop toxins from flowing away from the site (Carmichael, 2019).

Where did all the money go if the CLG never installed the groundwater treatment system? From what I could see, it was spent on lawsuits against contractors and others, lobbyists to fight state legislation, and efforts to prove they didn't need to fix the problem.

In the 1990s, it appears there was a lot of public debate and political maneuvering.

Some claimed that the state should foot some of the bill, not the local taxpayers. The dump was "Licensed by the state, inspected by the state, and approved by the state." The state had even ordered the dump to accept "the refuse from an oil spill cleanup. Why then should the state of New Hampshire… get away free?" (Favinger, 1990).

The powerful waste industry (i.e., Waste Management, Inc. and Browning-Ferris Industries), responsible for about 17 percent of the pollution, may have lobbied for relaxed regulatory action (United States Environmental Protection Agency—Region, I, 1991). For example, in 1988, Dr. Paul Connett, a chemist, asserted that New Hampshire's regulatory climate represented "The revolving door that exists between government and the waste disposal industry" (Young, 1988). Such a close relationship between regulators and the regulated is unhealthy for democracy and dangerous for its citizens.

Hank Cole, a scientist who worked for Clean Water Action, said in 1988, "It sounds like everyone is trying to avoid responsibilities for cleaning up this site [...]. There may even be collusion between responsible parties" (Young, 1988).

From the historical record, it does appear that there was a lot of maneuvering to avoid accepting responsibility for the remediation and health impacts. Taking responsibility, especially for cancers in children, would have exposed the polluter group companies and the agencies that oversaw the activities to liability and high costs.

But, if the EPA had forced CLG to implement the original plan decades ago, it may have protected seacoast residents from exposure and possibly prevented at least some of the children's cancers. So why did the EPA go back on its promise to protect public health? In the decades I had worked in the industry, I had never heard of the EPA overturning its selected remedy.

CLEARING OBSTACLES

I needed to find out what had happened. Why were we in the same position that Ms. Wylie and Ms. Martin had been in decades earlier?

I tried to access the CLG's files, but the CLG refused access. The polluter group was a hybrid entity since 63 percent of its funding came from taxpayer monies. The remaining 37 percent of the responsibility is shouldered by private entities including waste haulers Browning-Ferris Industries and Waste Management and generators[4] including Public Service Company of New Hampshire (now Eversource) and

---

4   EPA defines "generators" as parties that arranged for the disposal or transport of the hazardous substances (https://www.epa.gov/enforcement/superfund-liability).

Erie Scientific (Messmer et al., v. Coakley Landfill Group, 2018). Therefore, the files and activities of the polluter group should be open to the public. So, a group of activists and legislators filed suit in New Hampshire Superior Court (Messmer et al., v. Coakley Landfill Group, 2018) to access the historical documents. Attorney Paul Twomey spoke on our behalf, asserting that the public had a right to know how the group used the money.

The judge ruled in our favor: "As a hybrid organization, [CLG] is subject to New Hampshire's Right to Know Law and all meetings must be held in public, and all records must be accessible to the public" (Delker, 2018). After the court decision, due to a conflict of interest raised in our case, attorney Robert Sullivan continued in his role as the City of Portsmouth attorney but stepped down as chair of the polluter group, a position which he held for decades.

Did the EPA buckle to political pressure in New Hampshire and reverse the Coakley cleanup decision that has left us with a toxic mess in my community?

Very likely, based on what I have found.[5]

Our successful suit against the polluter group compelled public access to historical files concerning the dump. Several correspondences retrieved from those files detail the polluter group's attempts to exert political pressure on the EPA through US representatives and senators. For example, a July 1, 1994, memorandum from Seth Jaffe, the attorney representing the chemical generators' interests, wrote: "EPA won't be happy to hear from the Congressional delegation.

---

5   In 2021, I met Dr. Kyla Bennett, who had worked for the EPA when the EPA reversed the closure decision for the Coakley Superfund Site. Her story about her successful lawsuit against the EPA, discussed in chapter 6, provided that my suspicions about political interference were valid.

But, on the other hand, if we have good relationships with them, we could suggest they contact EPA without stating that they were doing so at our request."

According to correspondence that I found dated later in 1994, Congressman Bill Zeliff, US Senator Bob Smith, US Senator Judd Gregg, and New Hampshire Department of Environmental Services staff were communicating about the remedial plans for Coakley. A 1998 EPA letter to the CLG referred to a meeting in Washington, DC, and an agreement between the EPA and the State of New Hampshire to a phased approach to determine "whether Phase II of Operable Unit One [the active groundwater treatment capture system] was still necessary." A 1998 news article documented ongoing discussions between the CLG polluter group, the EPA, and the US Department of Justice. Justice Lois "Schiffer has expressed outrage that Sen. Smith's office had been contacted to resolve the matter." CLG asserted the remedy would be ineffective, and the cost was too high (Schreiber, 2010). In 1999, the EPA overturned the original cleanup remedy for the dump: "The groundwater extraction and treatment portion of the source control remedy specified in the ROD should be eliminated" (Meany, 1999).

The polluters won.

But even after I had obtained access to the files, I still had many unanswered questions. For example:

- How much of a threat does the dump pose to our community?
- Why did the agencies push back when I tried to get them to take action to protect the public?
- What happened decades ago that contributed to the continued pollution?

- Is it safe for my family to use our tap water?
- Where did the $17M go?
- How could I make sure the polluters clean up their mess at the Coakley dump?

My professional and advocacy worlds had collided, and I had to decide. Would I continue to work as a consultant or fully take on the advocacy role? As a mom of a child with significant health issues, albeit his prognosis was better than for the children with cancer, I understood the parents' pain and anxiety when confronted by their children's cancer diagnoses. While at first, the state did not want to notify the public of the cancers nor act, the task force shined a light on the issue. As a result, more cancer cases came to light and ripped the scab off a decades-old toxic dump primarily forgotten that threatened water supplies in five towns. Why was there so much pushback from agencies tasked with protecting us? Why were we in the same position as Ms. Wylie and Ms. Martin twenty-five years before us? As of the writing of this book, many of these questions remain unanswered.

Driven by a desire to compel action, I decided to step into a position that I would never have considered on my own.

CHAPTER 3

RUNNING FOR A CAUSE

—

"Women run for office because they want to accomplish something. They want to see a change in the hospital, they want to see something happen in schools."

—US SENATOR JEANNE SHAHEEN (BASH, 2017).

My first impulse was to say no when my state representative asked me to consider running for office. I had never considered doing something like that.

"I'm a scientist. Not a politician," I said.

"That's why we need you in Concord—we need scientists working on policy," my state representative said.

I was a nonconfrontational, shy person whose nerves made me physically ill before business presentations. I did not speak with the kind of hyperbole that I had become accustomed to hearing from politicians. As a scientist, I presented data and facts without emotion or exaggeration.

"Don't say no right away," he said. "Please think about it for a few days and let me know."

My community faced at least one enduring and substantial environmental threat. Unfortunately, the federal and state agencies tasked with protecting us tended to side with polluters who wanted to continue the status quo. They tried to keep slow-walking action if taking any at all. I had always felt that I did not entirely understand the political forces responsible for the failure of government agencies to address the cancer cluster investigation.

Everyone had kicked the Coakley pollution down the road, leaving us in virtually the same situation as Ruth Martin and Lilian Wylie decades before. I wanted to see the Coakley dump pollution stopped and controlled. Perhaps the best way to compel action is to propose laws. If nothing else, talking about proposals to pass laws could spur action.

Like most women, I am positive I would never have run for a political office if someone hadn't suggested it.

But was I qualified?

My immediate thought, like most women, was I doubted that I was qualified.

Women "need to be asked," said Sue Ellspermann of Right Women Right Now, an organization that recruits female candidates to run for office in Indiana. "Women are still not likely to just take that step on their own" (Keith, 2014). Dr. Brenda Major, a social psychologist at the University of California, Santa Barbara, said, "So many competent, capable women are basically selecting themselves out of leadership positions, and I think that we've all wrestled with this" (Keith, 2014).

Monica Youngblood said when asked to run for Congress, she thought, "Am I qualified to do this? Do we have the time? It will be a sacrifice, not only to my profession but my family, my kids" (Keith, 2014). Youngblood was elected to the US House of Representatives in 2014.

I considered the same issues when I processed whether to run for elected office. Part of me thought I should just continue to run my business, sitting behind my computer.

- Would I be able to put myself out there?
- Would I be able to convince people to vote for me?
- Would I be able to make them understand the importance of the issues?
- What would my kids think?
- Would I just embarrass myself and my family?

But I knew that environmental issues were at least part, if not a significant factor, of the health challenges my community faced. I thought people would see the light and agree with me if I communicated the science and facts. I knew if I was elected, I could try to make a difference by working on changes to regulations. I knew I could propose important policy changes that might force action if I won. So, to me, I had a responsibility to step up. I discussed my thoughts with my husband and sons. It could open me up to criticism, but my family might also suffer by association. A few days later, after thinking it over and discussing it with my family, I decided to do it. But I don't think any of us fully anticipated the changes that would result.

DISCOMFORT ZONE

As part of the campaign process, I participated in two candidate forums—one in my town and one in the neighboring town that also made up the district I would represent. I wore slacks and conservative, businesslike attire. I had no idea what the seating arrangements would be; I just knew I didn't want to worry about a wardrobe malfunction in front of a crowd of people, along with trying to concentrate on what I was saying. I was thankful I did because the table had no skirt around it.

To campaign, I had to step out of my comfort zone, go door-to-door, meet people, and strike up conversations with them. I debated contenders in candidate panels and raised a little money to buy signs, send letters, and make flyers. However, I never felt entirely comfortable with the tasks required to campaign.

Even so, on Election Day 2016, I got the call around 10:30 p.m. with the results: I had won the seat to represent my community in the New Hampshire House! While I was happy to have won, I was also nervous about entering the new world. I was in my kitchen, gathered with a few friends and supporters around our thirteen-inch kitchen television, watching the national election returns coming in. As I took the call from the town chair, the returns came from Florida, indicating that Trump was winning. After I hung up the phone, I felt worried instead of joy. My friends left with forced congratulations; we were all tense about a potential Trump presidency. Instead of attending any parties, I decided to go to bed, hoping that the Presidential election would just be a bad dream in the morning.

But, after I woke up, I turned on the TV while I made my coffee. The banner at the bottom of the screen read, *President-elect Trump.*

A DIFFERENT WORLD

On inauguration day, I was thrust into an entirely different world. There were four hundred state representatives, primarily men with an average age of about seventy years old, in the New Hampshire House. Women occupied only 29.5 percent of the House seats (National Conference of State Legislators, 2017). I assumed my temporary assigned seat in the historic Representatives Hall, among those with divergent political ideologies from my own. As a Democrat, I was a member of the minority party in the House. Republicans had also won the state governorship and a majority of the state senate.

As a younger scientist who ran as a Democrat from a predominantly Democratic area of the seacoast, I felt like an anomaly. I was overwhelmed by the day's events and the enormity of the tasks before me. Instead of making it through the complete list of inaugural after-parties at area bars and restaurants, I retreated to my hotel room.

As a member of the minority, I knew the math meant I had to get Republican votes to pass my legislation; therefore, I needed Republicans to understand my proposals. I decided the first step would be to convince the Senate Republican majority leader to help me by sponsoring the four bills I proposed. He agreed to meet with me, and we chatted about the rocks on his desk; we shared a common interest in geology and the outdoors, and he agreed to sign on to my bills. I thought maybe our chat about rocks helped. Since the senator signed on, it seemed to signal to other Republicans who also supported my bills. I developed good working relationships with some of the most conservative-leaning Republicans on environmental issues, even when we did not agree on any other topic. For example, I began working closely with Representative Jim McConnell, a Republican from Cheshire

County, who had strong convictions about chemical exposures based on his experience in the military. Nevertheless, my allegiances opened me to criticism within the Democratic caucus.

The Democratic party leadership in the House asked me to cut three of my bills. They thought I couldn't possibly handle all of them as a freshman. However, I had promised the voters I would do this work, and I had to follow through, so I ignored their request.

While my bills gained support from many Republicans, I was shocked when some Democrats opposed my legislation.

SWIMMING AGAINST THE TIDE

As a state representative, guided by science, evidence, concerns about climate change, and environmental exposures, I had to vote my conscience. For example, I could not support an antiquated steam-heating system for the City of Concord, an energy company boondoggle initiative. Nevertheless, the caucus lobbied for support with claims that it would create an emergency if the measure failed. It was clear though we needed better alternatives. I was one of only six Democrats who did not side with the caucus on this issue because I thought we needed to take steps to address climate change. First, we had to move away from relying on old, inefficient, fossil-fuel-based technology.

While trying to firm up support for my bill to limit PFAS chemicals in drinking water, I had a tense conversation with a Democrat from the Finance Committee. She said the state could not afford to pass strict protections on our drinking water for the "forever chemicals." She hung up the phone on me. I was shocked that some Democrats did not support clean water legislation to prevent cancer and chronic disease.

But a few years later, I would win a Democratic primary with a two-to-one margin over one of them, implying that the voters seemed to care about drinking water protection and cancer prevention.

POWER OF MONEY

My attempts to regulate pesticides, artificial turf, bottled-water labeling, and the safe levels of PFAS chemicals in drinking water garnered the most attention from state regulators, lobbyists, and the press. Lobbyists for DuPont, 3M, Saint Gobain Performance Plastics (Saint Gobain), Bayer, the International Bottled Water Association, solid waste disposal companies, and others roamed the hallways of the legislative office buildings of our tiny state. Lobbyists and other opponents would fill hearing rooms to watch the conversation and testify against my bills. Their attention far outweighed public members who voiced their support.

I worked on a critical environmental and public health issue in Merrimack caused by Saint Gobain, a Fortune 500 company with $43B in revenue in 2020 that had operated in Merrimack for decades. The industrial emissions belched from their stacks have polluted the drinking water in Merrimack and at least four other towns in Southern New Hampshire, and those citizens have a higher risk of cancer (Messmer et al., 2022).

However, the Republicans on the House Resources, Recreation, and Development Committee opposed the bill to regulate "forever chemicals." I thought it was worth trying to help them understand how important it was to protect their constituents from the pollution. Before the final committee vote, I approached the committee chairman, Chris Christensen, in the State House hallway. I presented a well-reasoned science-based discussion about the health studies that supported the need for regulation. He said nothing while I spoke, but after I concluded, he stated, "I don't believe you." I was shocked by his response. He questioned whether I was telling the truth? I could not sway his opinion.

When the bill got hung up in committee, a Senate ally helped add the PFAS drinking water protections as an amendment on a bill we gauged the House majority, and environmental regulators wanted to pass. However, this angered the Republicans and Merrimack legislators, and they walked away from the Committee of Conference, refusing to return for negotiations. The entire bill died.

I'M THE E-WORD

While my legislative proposals based on science and evidence targeted preventing exposure to chemicals and other products, the opposing parties began to level gender-coded attacks against me. One after another, lobbyists from the Business and Industry Association, the Municipal Association, and others called my bill "an emotional rush to enhance regulation and oversight" and wrote letters to the editor across the state claiming the attempts were based on emotion and "fear-mongering," not science. At first, I was shocked that in 2017 those lobbyists and regulators would resort to such misogyny. I never heard the same parties oppose legislative proposals brought by male legislators that way. But instead of being upset about the gender-coded attacks, I embraced the fact that I was emotional. I am emotional and passionate about preventing more families from facing cancer diagnoses. That emotion and a justified fear for my community, friends, and family drove me to run for office.

How could I not be emotional?

Children in my town and state died and were dying of rare, devastating cancers at significantly higher rates than elsewhere. In addition, adults were sickened with the nation's highest breast, bladder, and esophageal cancer rates (National Cancer Institute, 2020).

USING POLITICS TO CHALK UP A WIN FOR SCIENCE

In September 2017, I convinced my district's Republican senator to lead another attempt to pass robust protections for "forever chemicals" or PFAS in drinking water (Sen. Innis et al., 2018). Since he was facing re-election and the legislature and governor's seat were controlled by Republicans, I suspected having him as a lead sponsor might be the best way to get the bill passed. It worked. The bill passed, and the governor signed the act into law in 2018. As a result, New Hampshire became a leader in the nation for enforcing limits on four of the more than twelve thousand PFAS chemicals (U.S. Environmental Protection Agency, 2021).

Nevertheless, everything you do will be viewed as politically motivated when you are a politician. Behemoths like Saint Gobain, the Coakley dump polluter group, Waste Management, New Hampshire Municipal Association, and others fought my legislation. For example, I filed a bill to compel remediation and the polluter group to open their records to the public. Unfortunately, the Coakley Landfill polluter group attorney said, "There's been some pretty harsh politics lately surrounding the Coakley Landfill and the remediation. I have found it upsetting because it is not productive to reach a solution" (Sexton, 2018). Nothing could be further from the truth for me. Also, the male editor of the seacoast newspaper printed a libelous opinion piece, authored by a man, that attacked my scientific qualifications. How ironic that these three men could dismiss a woman's passion for protecting the environment and public health as only politics.

Politics was only a tool, a means to an end: to create healthier communities, which would benefit all. And I decided I could make more use of the tool.

HIGHER PURSUITS

In the fall of 2017, when Congresswoman Carol Shea-Porter announced she would not seek another term (Steinhauser, 2017), I was invited to a small meeting. I quickly realized the meeting was called to garner support for an older male's campaign to fill the open congressional seat, not to discuss who would be the strongest Democratic candidate. After the meeting, I walked out on the back deck and asked a woman who had been in the meeting, "Why shouldn't a woman run for this seat? A woman has been the Democratic candidate for this seat since 2006."

She answered, "Maybe you should run."

As a mom of two young men and a scientist, the existential threat that climate change posed made me feel I had an obligation to act. Our country and the world faced, and continue to face, significant existential threats and challenges with climate change and other environmental issues. The threats from climate change and science, in general, were substantial under the Trump administration. There was only one scientist, physicist Bill Foster (Dem., Ill.), in Congress at the time, and he said he felt lonely (Maron, 2018). I witnessed how important it was to create a science-based policy, so I decided to run for the open congressional seat to advocate for my children and future generations.

Many other scientists shared similar concerns to mine. A record number of scientists ran for Congress in 2018 to fight the anti-science and anti-climate change agenda of the Trump administration (Lavelle, 2018). Physicist Rush Holt, the chief executive officer of the American Association for the Advancement of Science, said, "Almost every issue that comes before the legislature has some science somewhere" (Lavelle, 2018). As a former congressman (Dem., NJ) for sixteen years, he had exemplified the importance of scientists' involvement in crafting legislation.

In New Hampshire, many people were interested and energized to support a scientist for office. Every chance I had, I tried to insert environmental and public health issues into the narrative of Democratic forums, explaining how important it is for scientist involvement in policymaking. As a result, our grassroots campaign garnered a lot of support.

But not everyone was supportive.

Social media was an effective tool for campaigning, but trolls posted lewd and nasty responses to my campaign posts. I routinely woke up at 5:00 a.m. or sometimes during the night to delete the comments, including vulgar expletives. It was shocking and added to the regular stress of running for office.

While I campaigned, people criticized my clothing, hair, and makeup (or lack thereof). This criticism was a surprise because this type of criticism of other women is outdated and unenlightened. I thought we had moved past this type of open criticism of other women.

While campaigning, I noticed that voters asked me questions that they did not ask the male candidates: How could I be a mom and a congresswoman in Washington? Other Democrats mansplained, accusing me of ulterior motives when I posted in a democratic forum about a critical science-related topic.

Another male candidate mansplained, accusing me of not being progressive enough about Medicare. Other male candidates aggressively attacked my platform and credentials. And another male candidate claimed he could have taken on my environmental platform, as I did. He asserted that my qualifications were nothing special, but he decided it would look bad for him, so he did not. Another candidate waged direct sexist attacks on my campaign. On my Wikipedia page, he had friends try to post "Her legislative accomplishments are minimal; she does not qualify under Wikipedia's criteria for scientists, consultants, or anything else." The I.P. address matched an office in Barnstable, Massachusetts, where the male candidate's college friend worked. He also got caught enlisting help from a relative to obtain private information from the membership staff at a union where I was a member. They told them I was a member in "good standing." But the union reached out to me to warn me of their attempts to get additional personal information. The party chairman reprimanded him, and I threatened to report him to the party attorney. Campaign events felt mainly like a boys' club. Some of the men also waged aggressive, sexist campaigning against another female candidate in the race.

After the filing date in June, eleven candidates had entered the race: three women and eight men. A few weeks before the primary, we solicited negotiations for the men to drop out of the race and support my campaign. We knew this would be a long shot; there had been tense relations between some of the campaigns. If we could gain the support of their voters, we might be able to overcome the monied interests of the other two candidates. Unfortunately, the men refused to drop out. None were realistic about their campaign's capabilities and support.

TAKING STOCK

By primary day, the two lead candidates had raised more than a million dollars. We raised about $200K, which was behind the two other leads but much more than the other eight candidates. My campaign won the third-highest votes, far ahead of the men who refused to drop out. It had been a family effort: Everyone had pitched in, making signs, and going door to door to ask voters to vote for me. Several months after, a political strategist asked me why I didn't know I would lose and drop out. Until the end, I thought there was a chance. Looking back, I don't think I could have waged a campaign as grueling as it was without genuinely believing I could have won until the very end.

Dr. Brenda Major, a social psychologist at the University of California, Santa Barbara, said, "Women have less confidence in their own abilities, judge themselves harshly—even when they are successful—and carry failures as more of a burden than men do" (Keith, 2014). I did judge myself harshly after the loss, but I have no idea if the men also judged themselves harshly.

But in 2019, I decided to run for the Executive Council, a unique elected executive branch body in New Hampshire, about a year later. That was another disappointing loss; after a two-to-one win in the Democratic Primary, I lost to a Republican in the general election.

Even though my bids for higher office were unsuccessful, campaigning allowed me to discuss the importance of science, climate change, clean drinking water, and cancer prevention. I also made acquaintances with federal representatives and so many people in the process who I would never have met any other way. Steve Marchand, a candidate for governor, said, "Mindi has brought protecting our drinking water to one of the top two issues people are concerned about in our state. Before she started advocating, the issue didn't even make it on anyone's radar."

I know that I would never have run for a political office had I not been asked. But my experience has shown me how important it is to include female scientists in policy decisions. Holding and running for office allowed me to become acquainted with the legislative process. I also met federal representatives and so many other people I would never have met any other way. In addition, campaign talks helped shape political discussions in New Hampshire and Washington, DC, on the importance of addressing drinking water protection and other environmental issues.

However, my experience running for office made me realize how much work still needs to be done to address gender inequity. I learned that running for political office as a woman is difficult due to gender norms that define politics as an old boys' club. As a result, politics is an atypical career choice for women (Werft, 2017). As Ritu Prasad quoted Dr. Kathleen Dolan, a political scientist on the faculty of the University of Wisconsin, Milwaukee, "Until we figure out ways to get more women to run, it's only going to be incremental change in their representation. From my perspective, that's the biggest challenge—getting more women candidates in front of voters" (Prasad, 2019).

We face significant global challenges. I couldn't help but wonder whether other female scientists encountered similar experiences. I had some questions:

- Have gender-coded stereotypes been applied to the scientific work of other female scientists and characterized their rhetoric as emotional, hysterical, or fearmongering?

- How have women historically been undermined and devalued based on their gender?
- Have we made any progress in the last few decades?

I decided to look at how gender stereotypes have historically challenged women to move forward. Unless we answer some of these questions and work to normalize women and female scientists, women will continue to be underrepresented in solving complex issues like climate change.

PART II

HOW'S IT GOING?

CHAPTER 4

WHEN WOMEN WEAR PANTS

—

"A woman accustomed to such work cannot be expected to know much of household duties or how to make a man's home comfortable."

—(LABOUR TRIBUNE, 1886).

I got up from my seat, finally.

After hours under the hot lights, fielding questions in front of a large audience, I was sweaty and gross, and my brain was fried.

Another night on the congressional campaign trail.

A woman was making a beeline for me. After several months, I had learned you never know what to expect.

She immediately yelled at me.

To my surprise, she wasn't upset about anything I said during the grueling forum. "Your hair looks terrible!" she screamed at me with an unhinged demeanor.

I was shocked and dismayed that she attacked me for my hair, of all things.

If that was all she got out of my presentation, I guessed I had failed to get my message across.

But the level and kind of criticism were a surprise when I stepped into the political arena. As soon as I did, without invitation, people started advising me on my clothes, hair, and makeup (or lack thereof).

I wasn't used to this kind of criticism.

INVISIBILITY

Growing up, I didn't care much about hair and makeup. I didn't feel like I belonged because the activities and interests promoted to girls as socially appropriate just didn't match my interests.

I liked to take apart telephones and put them back together rather than play with dolls. When I did play with dolls, I wanted to pretend they were preparing for and taking camping trips; I didn't put dresses on them or coif their hair. I liked to play touch football at lunch in junior high. After school, I enjoyed playing baseball, riding horses, and collecting rocks. In high school, I was interested in science and math.

At college, I dressed to fit in with men since most of my colleagues were male scientists. Like Forster, I tried to "dress as invisibly as I [could]. As a woman in science, I need to conceal my femininity to be taken seriously" (Forster, 2017).

In graduate school, a female professor who was at the top of her field wore jeans and flannel shirts all the time. She did not wear makeup and had a plain short haircut. My male colleagues jokingly likened her to Pat, the androgynous character from *Saturday Night Live*'s comedy show.

WHY SO MUCH FOCUS ON HOW WE LOOK, NOT WHAT WE SAY?

As I had personally experienced working my way through college and early jobs, men paid more attention to a woman's appearance and clothing than what she said or did. While writing this chapter, however, I learned of the long history of controversy about women's attire, specifically, about women wearing pants.

Unlike European women, women in central Asian cultures like the Ottoman Empire had worn pants or trousers for thousands of years (Micklewright, 2021). But Western authorities historically have cited Deuteronomy 22:5, "The woman shall not wear that which pertaineth unto a man, neither shall a man put on a woman's garment" to justify laws prohibiting women from wearing pants (Bain, 2019).

In 1841, a British commission investigating work conditions in coal mines in Staffordshire, England, uncovered dangerous and unsafe conditions in the underground mines for "Pit brow women" and child workers as young as five years old. Yet, news outlets and commission members focused on the women wearing heavy-duty trousers underneath skirts, like men's, jackets, and skirts rolled up, resembling aprons (Vintage Everyday, 2020). Even after laws were passed in 1842 prohibiting women from working in the coal mines, they continued to do so. Since women's wages were half of those paid to men, mine owners were willing to break the law to hire cheaper female labor, and they could always find desperate women to make sacrifices for their families (Frost, 2017).

In 1848, Columbus, Ohio, passed laws prohibiting cross-dressing sandwiched between laws that targeted prostitution and lewd public behavior (Eskridge, 1997; News

Desk, 2015). Between 1848 and 1950, forty-five additional US cities and towns passed laws prohibiting women from wearing the "dress of the opposite sex" (Tagawa, 2014), including an 1851 law in Chicago, for example (Eskridge, 1997; News Desk, 2015). According to Dr. Claire Sears, associate professor of sociology and sexuality studies at San Francisco State University, the laws were part of a broad crackdown on prostitution (Sears, 2014). Still, they became a tool for policing gender transgression. Many of the laws remained in effect for a long time: San Francisco's restriction on women wearing pants remained on the books until the 1970s. It was illegal for women to wear pants in France until 2013. The French law had originated in 1799, demonstrating that the French Revolution wasn't revolutionary in all things (Job, 2021).

Some women, however, pushed back historically, defying the laws that prohibited their wearing of masculine clothing and attempting to evade the gender pay gap or otherwise push for female empowerment. When France finally retracted its 1799 law banning women from wearing trousers in 2013, Najat Vallaud-Belkacem, the French minister of women's rights, noted that "The original law had been intended to prevent women doing certain jobs" (BBC News, 2013).

A pair of women garnered national attention with serial brushes with the law over cross-dressing. When interviewed in 1856, Harriet French showed that female dress and female pay were interrelated issues. She said that she and Emma Snodgrass dressed as men because they could "get more wages" (Kester, 2021). In 1851, female activists like Amelia Bloomer adopted early Ottoman pantaloons.

The suffragettes also adopted trousers to symbolize their movement, labeling them "freedom dress" (Chrisman-Campbell, 2019). This move of women suffragettes to wear trousers, however, garnered wide criticism as "A sign of moral decay and a threat to male power" (Chrisman-Campbell, 2019).

FREEDOM OF MOTION

Attitudes about women's clothing began to change in the mid-to-late 1800s. Generally, war provides greater opportunities for women to participate in the economy more actively and weaken traditional social conventions. We see this in the experiences of two women during the American Civil War and the Franco-Prussian War, Dr. Mary Edwards Walker and Jane Dieulafoy.

Dr. Mary Edwards Walker was the only woman in her graduating class from Syracuse Medical College in 1855. During the Civil War, she broke gender stereotypes by wearing trousers while working as a field surgeon. She refused a paid position as a nurse for the Union Army because she was a physician. She deserved an officer's commission. Instead, Dr. Walker worked in hospital tents as a volunteer and then as a contract civilian acting assistant surgeon who served on the front lines and even behind the lines (Lange, 2017). The *New York Times* reported that she "dressed in male habiliments" and carried "herself amid the camp with a jaunty air of dignity well calculated to receive the sincere respect of the soldiers" (Glakas, 2015). Dr. Walker refused to wear women's clothes from a young age, finding them "too restrictive and unhealthy" (Glakas, 2015), and was arrested several times for wearing men's clothes. In 1865, Dr. Walker became the first, and only woman ever awarded a Congressional Medal of Honor (Lange, 2017). But since she was never officially commissioned as an officer in military service, the award was later rescinded, although she refused to give the medal up. In her final act of nonconformance, Dr. Walker was buried in a black suit instead of a dress (National Park Service, 2021). President Jimmy Carter's administration restored the honor in 1977, fifty-eight years after her death.

Another female scientist, archaeologist Jane Dieulafoy, broke gender norms by wearing pants when she accompanied her husband as a sharpshooter on the front lines of the Franco-Prussian War. Ms. Dieulafoy, a French citizen who later became renowned for discoveries of ancient friezes and columns at the ancient capital of Susa in western Iran (DeRoche and Sanchez, 2020), opposed divorce as a devout Catholic. Dr. Rachel Mesch wrote that Ms. Dieulafoy's conservative views lessened her visibility as a controversial target: She was "never denigrated as a hysteric or a pervert, more likely labels for 19th-century women in pants" (Mesch, 2020). After Dieulafoy returned from Iran in 1886, she was awarded the nation's highest honor and petitioned the French government, which granted her full approval to wear pants (DeRoche and Sanchez, 2020).

Women have made progress and, in most countries, no longer must seek approval to wear pants. However, there is still a gender difference for girls who are told from a young age to watch what they wear to avoid distracting boys, while what young boys wear is not criticized. For example, a controversy erupted when dress codes were implemented for schoolgirls in a town outside of Dublin, Ireland, to avoid distracting male teachers (Casiano, 2020). Residents called the policy "sexist," and 6,700 signed a petition to push back on the policy.

Some think the root cause of the obsession with what women wear is rooted in objectification; since women hold little power, they submit to male prescriptions for their appearance (Barber, 2018). Others blame the media or instinct for the imbalanced attention on appearance between men and women. One study confirmed the influence of media and perceptions of media content plays a central role in activating harassment-related social norms (Galdi, Maass, and Cadinu, 2014).

Why is it important to women scientists how men perceive them? Some still think, "Women trade-off more power than men when they dress down, so women need to dress up to gain the same level of respect" (Tenure She Wrote, 2013). One study conducted in 2016 confirmed that for women pursuing careers in science, technology, engineering, and math (STEM) fields, "Feminine appearance may erroneously signal that they are not well suited for science" (Banchefsky et al., 2016). So, female scientists face a catch-22 dilemma; either way, they aren't taken seriously, no matter how they dress.

Female scientists face many subtle and not-so-subtle challenges with appearance and gender norms. For example, halfway through a marine arctic expedition, female scientists were told they "Could not dress in tight-fitting clothing due to safety concerns" (Oakes and Last, 2020). The new policy specified "no leggings, no very tight-fitting clothing—nothing too revealing—no crop tops, no hot pants [and] no very short shorts" (Oakes and Last, 2020). Several crew members were prohibited from contacting several women on the mission following reports of sexual harassment. Chelsea Harvey, a news reporter covering the trip, said the new rules "just triggered a lot of widespread resentment, this idea that women should have to be responsible for managing the behavior of men" (Oakes and Last, 2020).

BREAKING BARRIERS

Historically, women who challenged gendered appearance norms also cited the desire to earn higher wages. The gender pay gap persists, providing less opportunity for women to create a work and life balance while advancing their careers. In 2020, women made 81 cents for every dollar a man earned, and in 2021 they made 82 cents on every dollar (Payscale, 2022). The gender pay gap persists because women fill a disproportionate burden of lower-wage jobs; in 2020, women held full-time and part-time positions that paid wages at or below minimum wage at more than twice the rate of men (Statista Research Department, 2021). Women are overrepresented in many industries which pay their workers the least, like childcare, cleaning services, and restaurants (Rothschild, 2020). Women earn approximately 20 percent less than men for the same work; therefore, they must work one extra day per week or about an extra week per month to earn the same pay a man makes for the same work.

Evidence supports that when women are elected to political office, they are more likely to address the issues that underpin gender disparities. In states where women hold a higher proportion of elected positions, the gender pay gap is narrowed (Silver, 2014). However, women cannot contribute to female candidates to represent them with lower wages. "When women face significant barriers" to representation "the very basis of representative democracy is threatened" (Rothschild, 2020).

A record number of 589 women ran for Congress in 2018, and in 2020 women won 27 percent and 24 percent of the seats in the US House and US Senate, respectively (Blazina and Desilver, 2021). Even so, women are almost 51 percent of the population; therefore, women are still underrepresented in political office (U.S. Census Bureau, 2021). At the current rate, congress will achieve gender parity in thirty years (Rothschild, 2020). In addition, while 20 percent of the US population are women of color (Catalyst, 2022), only 11 percent and 2 percent of the US House and US Senate, respectively, are non-white women.

When they step into the political arena, female candidates experience challenges with fundraising (Rothschild, 2020). They also experience significant gender-based attacks while campaigning and during their tenure in office. For example, Congresswoman Alexandria Ocasio-Cortez (AOC) (Dem., NY), elected to the US House in 2018, was subjected to an avalanche of attention and criticism for what she wore or said. A *Washington Examiner* writer made headlines and spawned countless memes when he tweeted a photograph of Representative Ocasio-Cortez with the caption, *That jacket and coat don't look like a girl who struggles* (Del Valle, 2018). The congresswoman responded, "If I walked into Congress wearing a sack, they would laugh and take a picture of my backside. If I walk in with my best sale-rack clothes, they laugh and take a picture of my backside" (Greenberg, 2018).

Pennsylvania Congresswoman Madeleine Dean's mistreatment raised awareness about the misogyny of social media after she questioned US Attorney General Bill Barr during a House Judiciary Committee meeting in 2020 (Dean, 2020). Gender-coded attacks included calling the congresswoman an old hag, a bitch, and a witch.

"With the prevalence of the use of social media in campaigns and the divisive political climate, it seems there is a perfect storm of bold objectification of women in politics," stated Anna North (North, 2018). Continued pressure is necessary to force gender norms to evolve and for female scientists to be respected for their expertise and treated like their male peers.

POLITICS OF PANTS

At the start of this chapter, I shared my experience as a woman running for political office. As I learned, female politicians need to be more concerned about their appearance than their male counterparts to be trusted and taken seriously as candidates. One study suggested that when women wore revealing clothing it led to male perceptions that female political candidates were less honest and trustworthy and led to views that they were less competent or electable (Smith, et al., 2018). "Ever since women started holding political office, American men have been fixated on their clothes" (North, 2018).

Elected female members of the US Senate were not allowed to wear pants on the floor until 1993 (Foster, 2005). However, according to Associate Senate historian Don Ritchie, several female senators wore pants on the floor in the early 1990s; and after that, "Women could dress as they pleased" (Foster, 2005).

As a candidate for president in 2016, the press called Hillary Clinton's pantsuits "hideous," "unflattering," and "unfeminine." But the criticism turned into a symbol and rallying cry for female empowerment (Clemente, 2016). In response to complaints about Clinton's wardrobe, flash mobs of pantsuit-clad women danced in New York's Union Square. In addition, a 2016 pre-election Beyoncé concert included female performers dressed in white pantsuits (Clemente, 2016). "During the last election, I got endless calls to comment on Hillary's wardrobe. I said I would if I could discuss her male counterparts. No one was talking about what the men were wearing," said Vice President Kamala Harris (Adducci, 2019).

Since the 2016 election, female members have coordinated efforts to wear white or black pantsuits to display solidarity for women and family issues. In 2018, a record number of women and scientists—more than a dozen—ran for the US House and Senate to fight the anti-science and anti–climate-change agenda of the Trump administration (Lavelle, 2018). Congresswoman Rashida Tlaib (Dem., MI) said, "We're here. A lot of us have been out and about fighting for equal pay, fighting for Medicare—for all those things that I think are really important to women. Now we're actually at a place where women are making those decisions" (Lang, 2019).

When six women ran for the Democratic nomination during the 2020 presidential primary, they seemed to benefit from the path paved by Secretary Clinton. They wore pantsuits, skirt suits, and more casual shoes with very little, if any, criticism about their appearance (Adducci, 2019).

Kelly Dittmar, an assistant professor of political science at Rutgers University and coauthor of the book *A Seat at the Table: Congresswomen's Perspectives on Why Their Representation Matters*, states, "Media coverage of women's appearance and congressional rules around women's dress are a symptom of something bigger." Dr. Dittmar said both are indicative of "The fact that women still aren't completely welcome in the halls of government" (North, 2018). Dr. Claire Gothreau, a research associate at the Center for American Women and Politics, notes that criticism of women's appearance is a "tactic that has been used to delegitimize and diminish them" (Gothreau, 2020).

But objectification does more than just delegitimize. It also plays a causal role in gender harassment and sexual coercion (Galdi, Maass, and Cadinu, 2014). Gender harassment is a tool used by men who feel threatened by independent women who do not conform to gender stereotypes (Maass et al., 2003).[6] In addition, Dr. Gothreau said, "Objectification also has the potential to increase support for traditional gender role norms which would dictate that politics is not a place where women belong" (Gothreau, 2020). Vanessa Freidman, a reporter for the *New York Times*, wrote that "There is no question that fashion has been used as a tool to dismiss women; to associate them with frivolity rather than serious subjects—the superficial rather than the stuff of governance" (Freidman, 2020).

It's essential to understand the impact of media and social media on youth to break the cycle of establishing gender norms that lead to the objectification of women. A study conducted by Italian researchers suggests that media plays a significant role in perpetuating gender norms early. In turn, exposure to media provides "legitimacy to potential male harassers and [...] increase[es] the vulnerability of women and young girls as possible targets of sexual harassment" (Galdi, Maass, and Cadinu, 2014).

Objectification deters younger women and female scientists from entering politics. I asked Ms. Priya Shukla, an oyster biologist and doctoral candidate at the University of California at Davis, to consider running for office someday. Ms. Shukla said, "I don't see myself running for office, and to be honest, the reason is because of the mistreatment that AOC has experienced." First, they attacked her for "dancing on a roof, then they tried to make a full mockery of her and use unflattering photos."

---

6   Throughout this book, I refer to women or females; this is not intended to exclude members of the LGBTQIA+ community. Science is unfortunately typically presented in gender binary terms. There is a paucity of work examining factors that uniquely impact LGBTQIA+ scientists; significantly more research focus is needed.

But Shanika Amarakoon, an environmental engineer and woman of color, shared her thoughts about the 2020 New Hampshire Presidential Primary. Ms. Amarakoon said she thought to herself, "I am going to introduce [my daughter] to all the females because I just want her to think this is normal. And to this day, she asks why isn't Kamala Harris president?" Ms. Amarakoon said, "I think that's great."

While record numbers of women ran for congress in the last few years, and there is a female vice president and Speaker of the House, women are still only half represented, and it will take an estimated thirty years to catch up at the current rate (Rothschild, 2020). Gender norms for dress and wage inequity continue to devalue and suppress women in all fields, including STEM. Rather than evaluating female scientists for how they look or dress with gender catch-22 dilemmas, it is important to hear what they say and value their work.

I suspected that other female scientists were undermined or treated differently from their male colleagues, or their contributions were not fully recognized. What were the experiences of female scientists that laid the groundwork for female scientists today? Have we made progress recognizing the work of female scientists? I decided to examine the experiences of female scientists in the past to help make changes in the future.

CHAPTER 5

FEMALE SCIENCE PIONEERS

—

"Errors are notoriously hard to kill, but an error that ascribes to a man what was actually the work of a woman has more lives than a cat."

—HERTHA AYRTON, (MADAME CURIE'S
FRIEND (DES JARDINS, 2011)).

The widowed Dr. Marie Curie returned from a conference in Belgium to her home in Sceaux, Paris, with her daughters, fourteen-year-old Irène and seven-year-old Ève, to be greeted by an angry mob (Pasachoff, 2000).

The press had been vicious since 1910, when she had failed to be elected a member of the French Academy of Sciences by two votes. Her rival for the open seat, sixty-six-year-old Edouard Branly, was championed by French Catholics. The right-wing French press spread scurrilous and nationalist claims and gaslighted her, falsely claiming that she was

Jewish (Pasachoff, 2000). Physicist Émile Amagat claimed that "Women cannot be part of the Institute of France" (Des Jardins, 2011).

The press printed salacious rumors that she was having an affair with her lab assistant, physicist Paul Langevin. At the time, Langevin and his wife had been living apart for a year due to marital problems. The press asserted Dr. Curie was a homewrecker and claimed that the affair had started years earlier and driven her husband to commit suicide (the physicist Pierre Curie had died as a pedestrian in a traffic accident in Paris in 1906). In her autobiography, Dr. Curie's daughter Ève said the press called her mother "A Russian, a German, a Jewess, and a Pole, she was 'the foreign woman' who had come to Paris like a usurper to conquer a high position improperly" (Grady, 2017).

In the middle of the ordeal, the Royal Swedish Academy of Sciences awarded Dr. Curie a second Nobel Prize for her work in chemistry. Dr. Curie paid tribute to her deceased husband during her acceptance speech while spelling out their separate contributions to science (Des Jardins, 2011).

Dr. Curie had immigrated to France from Poland in 1891. She was the first woman to earn a doctoral degree in physics from the Sorbonne in Paris in 1893; the following year she earned a PhD in mathematics. Dr. Curie was the first female professor at the Sorbonne (Grady, 2017). Her first Nobel Prize in physics in 1903 had been awarded initially to her husband and another male scientist without acknowledging Marie for her pivotal role. The Swedish mathematician and advocate of women scientists, Magnus Goesta Mittag-Leffler, a nominating committee member, intervened on behalf of Dr. Curie. Pierre Curie also pressed the committee to recognize Dr. Curie's work, and it relented. As a result, Dr.

Marie Curie was the first woman to receive the prestigious honor. However, "When the prizes were awarded, Henri Becquerel was given 70,000 gold francs, while Marie and Pierre received a single sum of the same amount to share" (Heinecke, 2021).

All along, Dr. Curie had received criticism about being a bad mother since she spent most of her time in the laboratory. "It was difficult for traditionalists to imagine a husband and wife working side by side toward a common dream" (Heinecke, 2021). Despite her remarkable accomplishments, the fact that she was a woman in a man's field continued to serve as the source of discrimination for many jealous colleagues against her (Trombetta, 2014).

If not for the supportive men and women who were strong advocates, like Pierre, Dr. Mittag-Leffler, and Swedish female scientists, Dr. Marie Curie likely would not have received accolades for her important work.

MATILDA EFFECT

Dr. Margaret Rossiter, the author of the trilogy *Women Scientists in America*, examines the systematic under-recognition of female scientists, as experienced by Dr. Curie, from 1940 into the 21st century. In her book, Dr. Rossiter writes when contributions were overlooked it was "not due to any lack of merit on their part. It was due to the camouflage intentionally placed over their presence in science" (Dominus, 2019). She coined the term "Matilda Effect," named after the suffragist Matilda Gage, who first documented the predilection to attribute recognition to men instead of women (Berkshire Museum, 2022).

One glaring example of the lack of recognition for women's scientific contributions is the scarcity of Nobel Prizes awarded to women. Between 1901 and 2021, only fifty-eight of 975 Nobel laureates were women (The Nobel Foundation, 2022). Moreover, since 1901 only four Nobel Prizes for physics, seven Nobel Prizes for chemistry, and twelve Nobel Prizes for physiology or medicine have been awarded to women (NobelPrize.org, 2022). Shockingly, only four women of color have ever received a Nobel Prize, and none of those were for science (The Nobel Foundation, 2022).

SHE DISCOVERED THE FIRST DINOSAURS

A prime example of an early female scientist was Mary Anning, who was born in 1799 in Dorset, England. As a young girl, she learned how to find fossils from her father, whom she accompanied on expeditions (Newman, 2021).

When Anning's father died suddenly in 1810, she sold off her fossil collection to help pay off the family's debts. A year later, she discovered the first ichthyosaur skeleton with fossilized fish remains in its stomach (Eylott, 2022). Anning's other important discoveries included the first complete plesiosaur fossil and Britain's first complete fossil of a flying reptile, Pterodactylus (Newman, 2021). But, because it was unheard of at the time that a woman would be a geologist, her discoveries were credited to the men who bought the fossils. "She sold what she found. Her fossils are credited to the rich man who donated them to museums rather than the poor woman that found them [...]. Today, she would be running a department at Oxford or Cambridge," said David Tucker, the director of the Lyme Regis Museum (Newman, 2021).

Another female geologist, Katharine Fowler-Billings, was born and died in New Hampshire (1902–1997). She felt she had to "barge into a man's world," taking on a career in a field that was unsuitable for women (Aridas, n.d.). Dr.

Fowler-Billings's brother told her she was "too plain" to ever marry, but she married twice; the latter husband famed New England geologist Marland Billings (Aridas, n.d.). At a time when women could not, Dr. Fowler-Billings often dressed in men's clothing.

Dr. Fowler-Billings's story had many parallels to my life. She studied anorthosite in Wyoming (Bentley, 2020). My senior project at Syracuse was on Adirondack anorthosite. I still have some beautiful samples.

In retirement, she became a conservationist and environmental activist. Dr. Fowler-Billings died in Peterborough, New Hampshire, in 1997.

MALE ASTRONOMERS STOOD ON THEIR SHOULDERS

Many exceptional female scientists before 1950 owe their foray into science to their Quaker upbringing. Quakers encourage children, regardless of gender, to pursue their interests in science (Leach, 2006).

Maria Mitchell, a Nantucket, Massachusetts, native, is an example of a Quaker who made amazing discoveries in astronomy. Mitchell was born to an astronomer father and a librarian mother in 1818 (Narkhede, 2020). As Quakers, her parents supported her academic endeavors and encouraged her interests in science (Van der Does and Simon, 1999). After discovering a comet, Mitchell became the first female member of the American Academy of Arts and Sciences (Van der Does and Simon, 1999). In 1865, she became a professor of astronomy at Vassar College and one of the first female members of the American Philosophical Society (Maria Mitchell Association, 2022). In addition, she founded the Association for the Advancement of Women. Also, her work as a computer for the US Nautical Almanac made her one of the first female scientists to work for the federal government (Maria Mitchell Association, 2022).

Another female astronomer who followed in Maria Mitchell's footsteps was Dr. Vera Rubin, internationally known for discovering evidence of dark matter in the universe (Gallucci, 2016). After graduating from Vassar in 1948, Princeton University's astronomy doctoral program rejected Dr. Rubin because she was a woman; Princeton didn't accept women until 1975 (Soter and deGrasse Tyson, 2000). Instead, Dr. Rubin earned a PhD from Georgetown University in 1954 after attending Cornell University for a short time. Dr. Rubin was elected to the National Academy of Sciences for her pioneering discoveries and, in 1993, was awarded the National Medal of Science (Soter and deGrasse Tyson, 2000). But she was denied a Nobel Prize for her groundbreaking work on dark matter.

Astrophysicist Dr. Jocelyn Bell, who was born in Northern Ireland in 1940, credits her Quaker upbringing for her science career. Her parents "hit the roof" when her secondary school teachers tried to relegate the girls to cookery classes while the boys went to science classes (Proudfoot, 2021). "As Quakers, we believe there is something of God in everybody. Literally everybody. So, everybody needed a scientific education," Dr. Bell told the *New York Times* (Proudfoot, 2021). As mentioned earlier, gender equity in science education is central to Quakerism (Leach, 2006).

In 1967, Bell was a PhD student at Cambridge University in England, assisting astronomer Anthony Hewish, when she identified the existence of pulsars. This finding fundamentally changed our understanding of the universe. However, the world did not recognize her discovery. Instead of Dr. Bell, her advisor, Hewish, and the astronomer Martin Ryle were awarded the Nobel Prize for that discovery (Wu, 2018). "I think the fact that I was a graduate student, and a woman together demoted my standing in terms of receiving a Nobel Prize," Bell told the *New York Times* (Proudfoot, 2021). She also explained to *National Geographic* that in those days, "There was a senior man—and it was always a man—who had under him a whole load of minions, junior staff, who weren't expected to think, who were only expected to do as he said" (Lee, 2013).

THEY LAID THE GROUNDWORK FOR PHYSICS AND MEDICINE

As in other fields of science, female scientists have made important discoveries in medicine but, because of their gender, their work often wasn't recognized, or their accomplishments were attributed to male colleagues.

Microbiologist Dr. Esther Lederberg laid the groundwork for future discoveries on genetic inheritance in bacteria, gene regulation, and genetic recombination (Lee, 2013). However, due to sexism, her work was not recognized. Nevertheless, Dr. Lederberg's work provided the foundation for her husband, Joshua Lederberg's, Nobel Prize awarded in 1958. Unfortunately, Stanford University in California, where she worked until retiring in 1985, also denied her tenure (Marks, 2015). Her colleague Dr. Pnina G. Abir-Am said, "She never had a position commensurate with her position in science" (Steinmetz, 2019).

Dr. Rosalind Franklin was another scientist who deserved better from her male colleagues. She should have seen it coming when her new boss, Maurice Wilkins, mistook her for a secretary. From there, it went downhill. After Dr. Franklin was characterized as difficult to work with, some said she was treated poorly due to sexism (Jones, Reed, 2021). While working in Wilkins's laboratory, she identified and photographed the double helix structure of DNA and the genes inside (Jones, 2021). An archivist at King's College, Geoff Bowell, called Photo #51 "arguably the most important photo ever taken" (Walsh, 2012). Wilkins showed the photograph to James Watson, who used it without crediting Dr. Franklin when it was published (Watson and Crick, 1953).

Other female scientists who were trailblazers in physics and medicine are Lise Meitner, who made pioneering discoveries in nuclear fission, Chien-Shiung Wu (Lee, 2013; Drake, 2021), who worked on the Manhattan Project and made significant contributions in nuclear and particle physics, and Nettie Stevens, an American geneticist who discovered sex chromosomes (Lee, 2013).

THEY COMPUTED NASA'S TRAJECTORY

Women of color are underrepresented in science and often uncredited for their work. However, in 2016, the book *Hidden Figures* by Margot Lee Shetterly, which was the inspiration for the 2016 film *Hidden Figures* (Melfi, 2017), focused on three women of color who were "human computers" who worked for the National Advisory Committee for Aeronautics (NACA), the predecessor of NASA. Since most of the "human computers" were women, the term is dehumanizing and undermined credit for the female scientists' expertise and work.

The "computers" faced segregated restrooms and dining spaces while they were at work. For example, Ms. Miriam Mann, one of the computers, continued to take the "Colored Computers" sign off the cafeteria table and put it in her purse, considering it as a personal affront. Eventually, the staff finally stopped replacing it (Wei-Haas, 2016).

Human computers played a crucial role in performing calculations during World War II, and later their work propelled John Glenn, the first American astronaut to orbit the Earth, in 1962 (Howell, 2020).

Although the war caused strain on the labor market, few jobs existed for African Americans due to racial discrimination, regardless of gender. In 1941, under threat of large-scale civil demonstrations, President Franklin D. Roosevelt issued Executive Order 8802, which prevented racial discrimination in hiring for federal and war-related work. NACA hired an unknown number of black women they referred to as "computers" (Wei-Haas, 2016). Calling women "computers" dehumanized them and diminished their achievements until 2017. On June 1, 2017, eighteen people, including Ms. Mary Jackson, Ms. Katherine Johnson, and Ms. Dorothy Vaughan, were inducted into the NASA Langley Hall of Honor. NASA said the women "helped change the course history in aviation, space exploration, science—and even race relations" (Gillard, 2017).

Very little information is available about other NASA female scientists of color. Until Ms. Shetterly's work sifting through telephone directories, local newspapers, employee newsletters, stray memos, obituaries, wedding announcements, and the NASA archives, the work of the hundreds or perhaps thousands of black female "human computers" was unrecognized. Many women had short tenures at NACA, leaving their positions after only a few years due to societal pressures with marriage, childbirth, and child-rearing (Wei-Haas, 2016).

For example, Ms. Janez Lawson was the first African American woman hired into a technical position at NASA's Jet Propulsion Laboratory (JPL). Lawson had graduated from UCLA with a bachelor's degree in chemical engineering.

After working for NASA, Lawson went on to have a successful career as a chemical engineer (Greicius, 2016).

In the early 1960s, NASA trained thirteen American women astronauts and seven men for Project Mercury. However, even though the women completed the rigorous training, Congress decided that women could not fly in space and, therefore, they were never officially considered part of NASA (National Geographic Society, 2020).

SIDE EFFECTS

After World War II, there was an explosion of scientific research and ingenuity for American companies such as Goodyear and DuPont. The Manhattan Project that created America's first atomic bombs made science part of America's identity, and government funding poured into research. The 1950s brought the space race, the transistor, the structure of DNA, the polio vaccine, and Teflon™ pans (Zielinski, 2012). But there weren't enough consumer protections against dangerous industrial products or faulty pharmaceuticals.

Dr. Frances Oldham Kelsey saw severe issues with the drug Kevadon, known as thalidomide. In 1960, her first assignment at the US Food and Drug Administration (FDA) included reviewing the application for the drug. The German company that invented it as a cure for everything from insomnia to morning sickness touted that there were no side effects from the drug, and the medication was prescribed worldwide (Geraghty, 2001). However, at the FDA, Dr. Kelsey rejected the application for the drug's approval, citing a lack of clinical safety data and knowledge of preclinical studies she was part of in her postdoctoral training.

By 1960, Germany, the United Kingdom, Japan, Norway, and Canada were among twenty European and African countries that approved the use of thalidomide. The manufacturer began pressuring Dr. Kelsey and her bosses at the FDA to approve the drug. Dr. Kelsey did not cave to industry pressure—thank goodness she did not. In December of that year, a letter published in the *British Medical Journal* supported her concerns regarding extremity pain suffered by people on the drug (Geraghty, 2001). In the meantime, babies were born with unusual deformations of their limbs and ears. Finally, in 1961, a German pediatrician determined that the deformations observed in newborns were related to prenatal maternal use of thalidomide (Geraghty, 2001). As a result, the sponsor company withdrew its application from the FDA approval process in 1962 (Geraghty, 2001).

On Dr. Kelsey, President John F. Kennedy said, "Her exceptional judgment in evaluating a new drug for safety for human use has prevented a major tragedy of birth deformities in the United States" (McFadden, 2015).

BECOME A SCIENTIST?
GIRLS DIDN'T DO THAT SORT OF THING.

When she was eleven years old, Dr. Jane Goodall told everyone she wanted to go to Africa. From a very young age, she had an interest in apes. But everyone laughed at her; her family told her that girls just didn't live with animals in the forest (Stampler, 2017). Even so, at twenty-six, she got a secretarial job in Africa working for paleoanthropologist Louis Leaky with no college degree and no previous experience. The press called Dr. Goodall "the woman who redefined man" after her groundbreaking study of chimpanzees (Harrington, 2018). Her work prompted Dr. Leaky to sponsor her for a doctoral program at the University of Cambridge. In 1965, Dr. Jane Goodall was one of few to earn a doctoral degree in ethology without having a bachelor's degree (Stampler, 2017).

The media focused on her being a blonde while reporting her findings; yet her scientific methods were revolutionary for the time (The Springfield Union, 1964). She noted that she felt her gender made it easier for her to complete her work in Africa because "white males were still perceived as something of a threat, whereas I as a mere woman was not" (Goodall, 2018).

In 1986, Dr. Goodall became a full-time conservation and environmental activist. She expressed her frustration with politicians, "I don't think they've got the ability to imagine what this planet will be like if we continue to destroy the environment" (Harrington, 2018).

"ECOLOGICAL RADICALISM"

In 1962, Rachel Carson's *Silent Spring* (Carson, 1962) documented the adverse environmental impacts of overusing pesticides. Industry and the media dismissed Carson as an amateur, alleging that she did not understand the subject as a professional scientist would or that she distorted or misread the science.

Ms. Carson had a master's degree in biology from Johns Hopkins and had worked at the US Bureau of Fisheries for fifteen years. She was the second woman the agency had hired (Michals, 2015).

After *Silent Spring* was published, Secretary of Agriculture Ezra Taft Benson wrote a letter to President Eisenhower claiming that Ms. Carson was "probably a communist." Benson also wondered "why a spinster was so worried about genetics" (Lear, 1997).

The media reviews of Ms. Carson's book dismissed it as trivial, discounting her scientific background and using gender-coded stereotypes. *Time* criticized her "emotion-fanning words" and called her work "unfair, one-sided, and hysterically overemphatic" (Brooks, 1989). Velsicol Chemical Corporation, the manufacturer of the pesticides, including chlordane and heptachlor, threatened Houghton Mifflin, the publisher of *Silent Spring*, with a lawsuit over Ms. Carson's claims about its pesticides (Lear, 1997; Carty, 2012). In addition, the National Agricultural Chemical Association paid $25,000 for a public relations program against Ms. Carson's book (Stoll, 2020).

Ms. Carson accused the chemical industry of spreading misinformation and misleading the public about the safety of DDT and other pesticides. Critics described *Silent Spring* as "an essay in ecological radicalism that attempted to wake up a populace quiescent to the techno-scientific control of the world" and "one of the first scientists to bring ecological debate into the public sphere" (Kroll, 2002).

Ms. Carson testified before a congressional committee about the dangers of DDT in 1963 while she was dying from breast cancer (Flores, 2020). Her work led to a nationwide ban on the insecticide DDT. Some also credit Ms. Carson with spurring the creation of the Environmental Protection Agency (Lewis, 1985; Fahrenthold, 2007). "USEPA today may be said, without exaggeration, to be the extended shadow of Rachel Carson," said Jack Lewis.

After her death, President Jimmy Carter awarded Ms. Carson the Presidential Medal of Freedom in 1980 (Flores, 2020). Senator Ernest Gruening from Alaska noted, "Every once in a while in the history of mankind, a book [like *Silent Spring*] has appeared which has substantially altered the course of history" (Kamp, 2014). *Discover Magazine* named *Silent Spring* one of the twenty-five most outstanding science books of all time (Stoll, 2020). More than two million copies of *Silent Spring* have been sold (Griswold, 2012). Rachel Carson's crusade against the misuse of pesticides led to the founding of the EPA and other environmental organizations like Greenpeace and Friends of the Earth (Kamp, 2014).

Unfortunately, many more women deserve recognition for their groundbreaking work than presented here. Their pioneering work provided the foundation for all women to face future challenges. But women like Rachel Carson, Dr. Goodall, the talented female mathematicians and physicists from NASA, and others like them, broke gender barriers and prepared the foundation and roadmap for female scientists who followed their lead and boldly spoke out.

CHAPTER 6

NOBODY LIKES A SNITCH

—

"Zealous," he says, is "the kindest word I've heard used to describe her."

—JOHN DEVILLARS, (FORMER EPA REGION I ADMINISTRATOR) (JONAS, 2003).

Twitter trolls attacked Dr. Elisabeth Bik mercilessly, calling her a witch hunter, mercenary, crazy woman, nutcase, and failed researcher (Lee, 2021). The attacks were so vicious, unyielding, and unrelenting that she recently set her Twitter feed to private.

As a scientist, state legislator, public health advocate, and candidate for public office, I suffered similar gender-coded attacks on social media and in the press. Feeling compassion and empathy for Dr. Bik, I gave her my support and offered to share her story (NH Science and Public Health, 2022).

In 2020, US President Donald Trump proclaimed that hydroxychloroquine could be "one of the biggest game-changers in the history of medicine" (Solender, 2020). Didier Raoult, the director of the Mediterranee Infection Foundation, located in Marseilles, France, had conducted the study and reported the results in a renowned, peer-reviewed scientific journal (Lee, 2021).

Dr. Bik noticed something amiss in the study that skewed the results and made the drug seem more effective and less dangerous; the analysis removed people who had died or had serious side effects during the trial. The manipulation was serious and called into question the validity of the study. On her blog, *Science Integrity Digest*, Dr. Bik pointed out critical errors in the Raoult study that suggested that hydroxychloroquine provided no benefit for treating COVID-19 and might even make people sicker (Bik, 2020).

In July 2020, the FDA revoked emergency use authorization to treat COVID-19 with hydroxychloroquine, confirming Dr. Bik's assertions (Facher, 2020; Noack, 2021). In May 2020, the European Medicine Agency (EMA) warned that there was no proof the drug worked for COVID-19 and reported that some patients suffered serious side effects and fatal heart problems. As a result, the French government banned hydroxychloroquine for COVID-19 treatment in May 2020 (France24, 2020).

I have just been informed that an investigation has been opened following our complaint against Ms. Bik and Mr. Barbour.

SOCIAL MEDIA ATTACKS ON DR. ELISABETH BIK.

In April 2021, Raoult's collaborator, Eric Chabriere, messaged on social media that they had filed a criminal complaint against Dr. Bik in French courts. He tweeted a screenshot of the complaint, revealing her home address to the world (Lee, 2021). During an interview, Dr. Bik told me that the court did not act on the complaint. She told me that she felt Raoult's court filing was an attempt to intimidate her, to shut her up.

Social media trolls blasted her with rude comments about her age, appearance, body, and expertise. Dr. Bik said the attacks were misogynistic and different from attacks on male colleagues. Lonni Besançon, a French postdoctoral research fellow, agreed with Dr. Bik. He said he received multiple death threats after raising concerns about the Raoult team's hydroxyquinoline study. "But the attacks I get as a white man are a fraction of what women researchers and researchers of colour get," he said (Davey, 2021).

In response, over 2,200 scientists and thirty-two organizations signed an open letter stating that, "As scientists [we] stand up to protect academic whistleblowers"[7] in response to "the intense harassment of Dr. Bik by Prof. Raoult and some other members of his institute have responded by insulting her on national television, disclosing her personal address on social media, and threatening legal action for harassment and defamation. Prof. Raoult and his team's behaviour toward Dr. Bik and others have been pointed out by many international media outlets [...]. This strategy of harassment and threats creates a chilling effect for whistleblowers and for scholarly criticism more generally" (Besançon et al., 2021).

Since her original discovery, Dr. Bik told me that she had found potential ethical and misconduct issues in sixty-two other published articles authored by Dr. Raoult and the Mediterranee Infection Foundation. In addition, in a three-part series on her website, Dr. Bik published her concerns about image manipulation and the lack of proper ethical oversight in the studies (Scientific Integrity Digest, 2021).

In September 2021, the Mediterranee Infection Foundation announced that Raoult would leave in the fall of 2022. Although Raoult sought to stay on, Michèle Rubirola, the deputy mayor of Marseille who oversees public health, said it was "Time to turn the page [...]. You have to have the humility to acknowledge that you've been wrong" (Noack, 2021).

---

7   A whistleblower is a person who exposes information or activity, within
     a private, public, or government organization, that is deemed illegal,
     immoral, illicit, unsafe, fraud, or abuse of taxpayer funds.

Dr. Bik continues to examine studies; she identifies issues in about 4 percent of journal publications (NH Science and Public Health, 2022). The ripple effect could be enormous since thousands of other papers cite them. To date, she has identified issues or misconduct in more than five thousand other scientific studies that resulted in 594 retractions and more than 474 data corrections in publications by other authors. However, she told me that most of the studies had not been publicly addressed or retracted by journals' editorial boards. Dr. Bik offered that retracted papers are more likely to have male last authors; men hold the top thirty-one positions on the Retraction Watch leaderboard (Abritis, Marcus, and Oransky, 2022).

In December 2021, Dr. Bik was honored with the "John Maddox prize for standing up for science in the face of harassment, intimidation, and lawsuits." In her acceptance statement, Dr. Bik noted that "the intense pressure to publish papers is leading to a 'dilution' of the quality of scientific literature" (Devlin, 2021).

1950S PLAYBOOK SEVENTY YEARS LATER
As we saw in the previous chapter, the release of Rachel Carson's book *Silent Spring* in 1962 unleashed a tidal wave of sexist attacks. The press used gender-coded terms like "spinster," "hysterical," and "emotional" to undermine her scientific credibility. It's unfortunate that almost sixty years later, in 2020, Dr. Bik experienced similar blowback when she exposed misconduct by a male researcher. As discussed in previous chapters, regulators also used gender-coded attacks to intimidate or silence me.

In 2020, a sexist *Wall Street Journal* op-ed called for Dr. Jill Biden to drop the "Dr." because she was not a medical doctor. The attack encapsulates how female scientists are undermined by gender-coded stereotypes and micro-aggressions. The controversy resulted in significant pushback from female scientists (Kindelan, 2020).

"The playbook for undermining female whistleblowers relies on the same '1950s stereotypes' used to target any woman who speaks out," stated Dr. Veena Dubal, who studies labor, race, and gender issues at the University of California's Hastings College of Law. Women who speak out "get so much harassment," she said. "They are not believed. They are seen as hysterical, as angry, as unqualified" (Booker, Birnbaum, and Nylen, 2021).

In this chapter I share more stories of contemporary courageous women who pushed back to protect public health and the environment, paving the way for people like Dr. Bik and me who saw a public health threat and acted.

TAKE HER SERIOUSLY

While working at the EPA in the 1990s, Dr. Kyla Bennett told me she struggled with constant gender-related micro-aggressions. At the time, Dr. Bennett had a PhD in ecology and evolutionary biology and a law degree.

While at the EPA, she also had to suffer the professional indignity of listening to the drunken voice messages her boss had left her, detailing his explicit sexual desires and professing his love for her. This story resonated with me because, as a young female scientist working in a male-dominated firm around the same time, a superior asked me to come to his hotel room one night to "work." Such proposals went with the territory of being a young female employee in male-dominated fields like science. Neither Dr. Bennett nor I reported the problems higher up the male-dominated hierarchy.

When I spoke with Dr. Bennett, she shared, as a petite female scientist, "You're not taken seriously. Ever."

Dr. Bennett reviewed a permit, while at the EPA, that conflicted with wetlands regulations. She told me, "It was a horrific case that would destroy the wetlands and eelgrass on the island." Sears Island was part of undeveloped coastal Maine located at the head of Penobscot Bay (U.S. Department of Transportation Federal Highway Administration, 2020). Dr. Bennett knew that an equally destructive development project had earlier been proposed for the island (Platt and Kendra, 1998). The significant pushback it faced from environmental advocacy groups and the public resulted in the United States Department of Transportation (USDOT) abandoning that earlier project, citing environmental and economic infeasibility.

In 1994, Dr. Bennett told her boss that she couldn't approve another plan to destroy the island. He replied that US Senator George Mitchell wanted the Sears Island permit application to be approved. "If she didn't do it, he would find someone else who would." Dr. Bennett told me, "I refused, so he took me off the case." She sought help from Public Employees for Environmental Responsibility (PEER). With PEER's help, Dr. Bennett filed a whistleblower complaint with the Department of Labor (Jonas, 2003). According to Dr. Bennett, when that agency sided with her, "The EPA capitulated immediately. The permit was never issued. The island is still undeveloped. And I got to keep my job although they switched me over to enforcement."

In 2001, Dr. Bennett went to work for PEER as its New England director. The organization has continued to support public employee whistleblowers now for twenty-five years. Dr. Bennett said that about half of their PEER clients are women. For her part, Dr. Bennett said, "I don't enjoy being labeled a troublemaker, but I have come to accept it. It's the business we're in" (Jonas, 2003).

Although her former boss at the EPA, DeVillars, called PEER "a fringe group bordering on irrelevant" (Jonas, 2003), Dr. Bennett works extensively with EPA whistleblowers. In the past year, six out of seven toxicologists who work in the EPA's new chemical approval department exposed issues with management (Lerner, 2021d). The jobs of these whistleblowers, who hold doctorates in toxicology, chemistry, biochemistry, and medicinal chemistry, were to assess and identify potential harms posed by new chemicals (Lerner, 2021). The six complaining EPA toxicologists allege that managers pressured them to minimize or remove evidence of potential adverse effects of the chemicals, including neurological effects, congenital disabilities, and cancer, to get the chemicals approved by the EPA. As a result, the EPA scientists say that more than half of the 368 new chemicals submitted for approval in 2020 could pose risks of varying significance, even though the agency determined risk as "negligible" (Lerner, 2021c). After seven months of no response from managers, the scientists filed a complaint against the agency (Lerner, 2021).

Repercussions for being whistleblowers followed. EPA managers reprimanded the whistleblowers for not reviewing new chemicals quickly enough. When Dr. Elyse Osterweil found atypical and severe toxic effects in rats exposed to one chemical, she said her supervisor told her, "Why don't you take a look at the actual study data again, and maybe the hazards will go away" (Lerner, 2021). Dr. Osterweil stated that when she refused to alter her findings, her supervisor gave her negative performance reviews, writing that she had a "pattern of providing late and incomplete work products" (Lerner, 2021b).

Dr. Sarah Gallagher's supervisor claimed that she had difficulty "letting go when a decision was made" about a particular chemical. "We started getting increasing pressure to use the wrong exposure metrics," said Dr. Gallagher, who holds a PhD in toxicology. The EPA reassigned her to another office a month after refusing to revise her work (Lerner, 2021).

According to Dr. Bennett, female scientists in the EPA's chemical approval agency may still have some of the same issues she experienced in the 1990s. She shared that female EPA scientists with doctoral degrees are repeatedly undermined. EPA managers, industry representatives, and consultants do not address the female scientists with doctoral degrees as "Doctor," they call them "Ms."

In October 2021, the new EPA administrator, Michael Regan, came to Merrimack, New Hampshire, where I met him. When I asked him how the agency would address the whistleblowers' complaints, he became visibly angry and stated that their assertions were not the whole story and that we would soon hear the EPA's side. Unfortunately, his response didn't engender confidence that he would address the management issues.

ARE WOMEN MORE LIKELY TO BLOW THE WHISTLE WHEN THEY SEE SOMETHING WRONG?

Dr. Kyla Bennett told me, "Virtually all whistleblowers do it as a last resort because they are so afraid of what's going to happen to human health, the environment, or a particular species. They just can't look in the mirror every morning and not act."

"I think women's tolerance for bullshit is just a bit lower," said Bianca Goodson, a whistleblower, and the former CEO of Trillian Management Consulting (Blackman and Dall, 2021). Goodson had exposed corruption between the government and McKinsey and Eskom in South Africa (Blackman and Dall, 2021).

Goodson and others suggest that since more women have risen to higher ranks within organizations in recent years, they are now increasingly in positions to observe and report wrongdoing. But even in more elevated positions, many may still feel like outsiders, which is at least part of why they feel obliged to report misconduct. "If you're not part of the boy's club, maybe that makes it a little easier to take a big risk," said Jessica Uhl, a friend of Sherron Watkins, the former vice president of Enron Corporation, who blew the whistle on its financial scandal in 2001 (Vulliamy, 2002).

The examples above and my own experience speaking out led me to believe that there is not much improvement in acknowledging and respecting female scientists for their contributions. Even though decades have passed since Rachel Carson's book was published, female scientists still face similar gender-based tropes and a lack of recognition for their expertise.

DO WOMEN SUFFER FROM RETALIATION MORE THAN THEIR MALE COUNTERPARTS?

The expertise of female scientists works against them when they raise concerns about public health threats. Micro-aggressions, aggressive micro-managing, inordinate negative performance reviews, and assignment to lesser positions are retaliatory measures against female scientists working at the EPA and other institutions.

Dr. Bennett said that while there are always challenges from one administration to another, Trump's presidency was the most dangerous threat to science and public health in American history. Female scientists spoke out in great numbers under the Trump administration about injustices relating to the COVID-19 pandemic and blatant attacks on scientific integrity, federal agencies, and national security. The Government Accountability Project launched a campaign entitled "Women Whistleblowers in the Trump Era: A Celebration of Women Who Refused to Be Silenced" that highlighted female scientist whistleblowers (Government Accountability Project, 2022). The website highlights female climate scientists like Maria Caffrey, who was forced out of her job in the National Parks Service when she refused to remain silent when all references to human-caused climate change were removed from her study by the Trump administration (Government Accountability Project, 2022).

One study analyzed how women who blow the whistle experience different retaliatory responses than men (Rehg et al., 2008). The study grouped the situations into two categories: the Social Role Theory and the Status Characteristics Theory (Rehg et al., 2008). The study found that bias may be a factor in the retaliation women experience when they expose wrongdoing.

The Social Role Theory predicted that when women violated expected gender norms, the level of retaliation was proportional to their role in society. Since whistleblowing involved exposing wrongdoing and not acquiescence, it is a "greater violation of role expectations for women than men. [W]omen who blow the whistle behave in a way that is inconsistent with their role as women and are likely to be more severely punished for this behavior than are men, for whom whistleblowing may be viewed negatively, but not as role inconsistent" (Rehg et al., 2008). In addition, women are expected to act altruistically but, whether they are altruistic or not, their actions engender negative responses. For men, altruism is optional, and they are less likely to suffer adverse reactions for not acting (Heilman and Chen 2005). So, either way, women are viewed negatively for blowing the whistle.

The Status Characteristics Theory assumes that whistleblowers suffer retaliation because of their hierarchal position in the organization. A person with a higher perceived position of power and status generally experienced less retaliation (Rehg et al., 2008). For men, standing in the organization is related to the level of retaliation. In contrast, the retribution for women seemed the same regardless of their position within the organization or the level of seriousness of the wrongdoing they reported (Rehg et al., 2008).

In addition, the more retaliation, the more likely women— but not men— were to say they would blow the whistle again, using external channels. Interestingly, the study by Regh et al. (2008) also found that both men and women reported that perceived retaliation "almost always occurred before external reporting and rarely occurred afterward." Women who experience retaliation are more likely to seek external channels for reporting when they suffer reprisal than men were.

Of course, federal and state laws protect whistleblowers who may experience retaliation when they speak out. But...

ARE WHISTLEBLOWER PROTECTIONS STRONG ENOUGH?

Whistleblower protections are more important for women since they experience more retaliation and have more to lose since they are paid a fraction of each dollar that men earn.

Every state and Washington, DC, has one or more whistleblower protection statutes covering state and business employees (West and Bowman, 2020). These protections vary from state to state, but each provides some level of legal protection for staff who report illegal and unethical wrongdoing.

In general, state laws require careful documentation of alleged violations and confidentiality for whistleblowers and the information they convey. But anonymous reporting is not permitted in state worker settings to the extent it is allowed in the private sector. In addition, appeal remedies are potentially available after case resolution, and most states have penalties for retaliation.

The federal *Whistleblower Protection Act*, initially passed as the Civil Service Reform Act of 1978, was amended four times: in 1989, 1994, 2012, and 2017. It protects federal employees who "believe there has been a violation of the law, rules, or regulations [...] or a substantial specific danger to public health and safety" (National Whistleblower Center, 2022). The 1989 act created separate entities to provide greater protections for whistleblowers: the Office of Special Counsel (OSC) from the US Merit Systems Protection Board (MSPB). The OSC's primary goal is to investigate retaliation complaints reported by federal agency whistleblowers and protect them from prohibited personnel practices. As currently written, the law provides protection if one is wrongfully dismissed or suffers retaliation. After employees exhaust administrative steps, they are entitled to a jury trial under the law (Temin, 2020). In addition, EPA employees can file a complaint to the Inspector General, an independent office within the EPA. Although the Inspector General's office is technically part of the EPA, the agency gets its funding appropriations separately from Congress.

"Justice delayed is justice denied."

—WILLIAM E. GLADSTONE

However, state laws do not protect federal government employees. The MSPB is the only avenue for a remedy for federal employees who are whistleblowers. Since that board has not had enough members to establish a quorum for five years, it has been unable to issue rulings (Alms, 2022). The result is an appeal to a single administrative law judge or, at most, a three-person panel of the MSPB. In September 2021, the MSPB had a caseload backlog of about 3,300 cases. According to MSPB reports, the board processes about one thousand cases per year, which means it will take more than three years to work through the current caseload (Bur, 2021).

A study conducted by the Office of Special Counsel in 1993 found that about 93 percent of federal employees believed that protection from retaliation was inadequate (U.S. Government Accounting Office, 1993). Additionally, about 90 percent of survey respondents thought their agency had little or no support for protecting federal employees from retaliation for reporting misconduct (U.S. Government Accounting Office, 1993).

As a result, many of the cases never make it to the MSPB in the first place. For example, another study conducted in 1993 found that of thirteen thousand government employees surveyed, only half who were aware of misconduct reported it. Thirty-seven percent of those who did report misconduct reported suffering retaliation. Nearly half (47 percent) of them said the reprisals took the form of poor performance appraisals (U.S. Merit Systems Protection Board, 1993).

The Office of Research Integrity (ORI) is one avenue for scientists employed by the Department of Health and Human Services to report whistleblower claims. The ORI oversees the scientific integrity and misconduct allegations on behalf of the Secretary of Health and Human Services except for the Food and Drug Administration (FDA) employees. But a report in 1995 indicated that only half of the employees who knew about agency misconduct reported it to the ORI (Office of Research Integrity, 1995).

POLICY NEEDS

Since many do not report wrongdoings, it is essential to examine policy shortfalls to preserve the ability to blow the whistle, especially for women who experience more retaliation than men. Whistleblowing exposes institutional problems and constructive criticism for organizational improvement (Miceli and Near, 1992). Streamlining and protecting the process for whistleblower complaints would also improve outcomes and reduce frustration with the process. Additionally, mandatory training for supervisors on handling retaliation complaints is required, and mandated disciplinary action for supervisors who violate certain protections. Formal policies should also be reviewed and proposed, as necessary, regarding the steps required to review and correct the issues raised by whistleblowers within federal agencies.

According to *The Intercept*, the EPA whistleblowers' complaints filed in 2021 were quickly and widely circulated within the EPA (Lerner, 2021a). Revealing their identities within the agency exposed the scientists to possible retaliation from management. Whistleblower complaints are supposed to be kept confidential. Dr. Bennett raised concerns about disseminating complaints within the EPA: "The fact that the EPA released our clients' names is inappropriate and troubling. They've been put in an incredibly uncomfortable situation" (Lerner, 2021). Managers involved in exposing the complaint should face penalties and be removed from their positions, if appropriate, to protect the process. In addition, Congress should strengthen agency policies to preserve whistleblower confidentiality.

Congress must ensure a quorum on the MSPB. David Colapinto, founder and general counsel of the National Whistleblower Center, stated, "Everybody has known about it for at least twenty-five years, and Congress has attempted to fix it several times" (Temin, 2020). Unfortunately, the problem has persisted regardless of what political party controls the White House or Congress. Colapinto noted, "This is really a breach of faith with federal employees for Congress to tell us in 2012 when they passed the other law that the administrative remedies will work [...]. And now there is no way that this system is working" (Temin, 2020).

Female scientists like Rachel Carson, Dr. Bik, and I feel a sense of duty to report when we see something amiss. That is "because researchers are professionals who have received training, education, and benefits from society, they have an implicit contract with society" (Shrader-Frechette, 2000). We feel a personal responsibility to speak out when we see something threatening public health. Unfortunately, because we violate social norms in the process, female scientists face aggressive gender-based attacks.

We must normalize, respect, and acknowledge women as scientific leaders so we can employ them as a resource to help solve complicated challenges like climate change and not just fritter away their time and talents having to protect their careers against bureaucratic injustices.

CHAPTER 7

WHEN WOMEN LEAD

—

"If they don't give you a seat at the table,
bring a folding chair."

—SHIRLEY CHISHOLM

Dr. Tom Ballastero, a professor from the nearby University of New Hampshire, stood up before the crowded North Hampton, New Hampshire, town hall meeting and recited words directly from a 1990s-era EPA report. The report he cited meant that the Coakley Superfund dump threatened all nearby towns' public and private water supplies. Packed into the room were residents, state regulators, EPA officials, and representatives of the polluter group.

In response, a male EPA representative gushed about how thankful he was to Dr. Ballastero for his time and work. And then Gerardo, the EPA manager, listened to the professor respectfully, never once interrupting to correct his interpretation or otherwise challenge any of his points.

I couldn't believe my own eyes and ears.

State Representative Renny Cushing of Hampton turned to me and said, "That's what *you've* been saying."

It was nice to hear from Representative Cushing's comment that he recognized how the regulators had earlier treated me. It was easy to think I had been too sensitive or that I had imagined the inequitable behavior. "Yes," I replied. I had said the same things but had received an opposite response from the male regulators many times before.

As discussed in Chapters 2 and 3, the regulators had tried to stall action and alleviate public concern about the toxic dump every step of the way. Every time I made the same points that Dr. Ballastero said in the last few years, I was rudely interrupted by Gerardo. The EPA manager had always asserted that toxic chemicals did not flow into all towns around the dump, a fundamental fact that even a fifth-grader would understand; that water (and the chemicals in it) flowed downhill. The regulators didn't want hundreds of people to know that the Coakley Superfund dump threatened their drinking water.

But I violated typical gender norms by leading the effort to educate and thus empower my neighbors, and regulators used those gender stereotypes to undermine my expertise and efforts. The regulators, all men, used the same approach from the 1950s-era playbook in earlier attempts to undermine Rachel Carson's activism.

I looked for other examples of gendered treatment of female scientists to see how they responded and perhaps learn from their experiences.

Did other female scientists suffer consequences when they led investigations, violating societal norms for women?

Unfortunately, the answer is **yes**.

Dr. Kirsty Duncan was appointed to be Canada's first minister of science by Prime Minister Justin Trudeau (McKenna, 2015). But she had to struggle against stereotypical challenges presented by male colleagues.

HEELS AND LEGGINGS

In 1998, Dr. Kirsty Duncan violated typical gender stereotypes when she formed a multidisciplinary team, composed chiefly of men, to retrieve samples of the virus that had caused the 1918 worldwide influenza pandemic. She thought the virus had possibly survived in frozen bodies buried in permafrost on a Norwegian island. Dr. Duncan, a medical geographer and author of *Hunting the 1918 Flu: One Scientist's Search for a Killer Virus*, put together a team of sixteen men, almost all older than her, with distinguished careers in various scientific fields, from geology to virology. Dr. Duncan handpicked team members: she knew the expedition would be complex, and she needed a wide variety of experts to be successful.

Dr. Duncan faced immediate hurdles and countless ego battles with male team members. They tried to put up roadblocks, steal glory, squabble over who deserved credit for fundraising dollars or scientific finds, and fought about where funding would go (the power lies with the institution that possesses the money). Team member Dr. John Oxford, a professor of virology at the Royal London Medical College, characterized Dr. Duncan as "exotic" and "young and rather good at Scottish dancing and weight-lifting" (Oxford, 1998). He didn't characterize Dr. Duncan as a scientist or that she was smart and capable. An article written by Oxford's daughter described Dr. Duncan as young and manipulative and dismissed her for "wearing a short skirt/ latex leggings/sexy suede and high heels at the graveyard" (Oxford, 1998).

Two mass-market books that described the expedition, Gina Kolata's *Flu: The Story Of the Great Influenza Pandemic of 1918 and the Search for the Virus That Caused It* and Pete Davies's *Catching Cold: 1918's Forgotten Tragedy and the Scientific Hunt for the Virus That Caused It*, characterized Dr. Duncan as passionate but unserious (McKenna, 2015).

Dr. Duncan continuously fought against the "sharp elbows and obvious sexism" and men who attempted to shut her out of her own investigation (McKenna, 2015). When the bodies of the influenza victims were finally unearthed and discovered to be "gooey" because of thawing, likely due to warming permafrost conditions and climate change (McKenna, 2015), Dr. Duncan's rivals quickly reported to the press that the mission had failed. But in 1999, Dr. Duncan refuted the claims reporting that "the tissue samples that people had dismissed as so bad are yielding very good results. We have fragments of the flu's genetic material, the RNA, from the lung, the kidney, the liver, and the brain" (Cox News Service, 1999).

Dr. Jeffrey K. Taubenberger had initially been an advisor on Dr. Duncan's team but emerged as a bitter rival (McKenna, 2015). Dr. Taubenberger and his team sequenced the 1918 viral genome from banked lung tissue samples obtained from a service member who died in South Carolina (Jordan, 2019) before Dr. Duncan's team could retrieve samples from Norway. The media coverage for Dr. Taubenberger's team was much more positive than for Dr. Duncan.

Then, at a 1999 conference, when Dr. John Oxford tried to take credit for the Duncan team's efforts and exclude Canadian scientists, Dr. Duncan herself arrived to state her case forcefully (McKeague, 2003). She eventually had another book published, *Environment and Health: Protecting our Common Future*, and served on the Intergovernmental Panel on Climate Change (IPCC) before being the first minister of science in Canada (McKenna, 2015).

What can we learn from Dr. Duncan's story?

Almost none of the accounts of her project considered the male scientists' appearances or clothing or criticized their actions in stereotypical ways. If Dr. Duncan were a man, she likely would not have had as many issues leading the team. But by focusing on the work and forthrightly protecting her reputation, her leadership qualities earned her recognition.

Why is this significant?

In 1999, Dr. Nancy Cox, the chief of the influenza branch of the CDC, noted, "It's important to know why the virus was so lethal," so we are prepared for the next pandemic (Cox News Service, 1999). The COVID-19 pandemic has shown us how important it is to design antiviral drugs and vaccines for pandemics and epidemics. We need the tested leadership and expertise of all relevant scientists, both women and men, to help us face down the threat of the next pandemic.

WHY ARE FEMALE SCIENTISTS PUNISHED FOR LEADING?

As discussed in Chapter 6, the Social Role Theory states that women who violate social norms are more likely to get pushback (Rehg et al., 2008). My own experiences with the EPA, like Dr. Duncan's, featured criticism from men that contrasted with the positive responses accorded to male scientists in the same situations.

According to Dr. Marianne Cooper from the VMware Women's Leadership Innovation Lab at Stanford University, women elicit pushback from others when they violate gender stereotype expectations for behavior. For example, Dr. Cooper said, "Women are expected to be nice, warm, friendly, and nurturing. Thus, if a woman acts assertively or competitively and pushes her team to perform by exhibiting decisive and forceful leadership, she is deviating from the social script that dictates how she 'should' behave" (Cooper, 2016).

Both Dr. Duncan and I had to overcome the gender-norm hurdle to accomplish our scientific goals, which set us up for more violations of societal norms. These are hurdles that male scientists do not encounter. Studies confirm the idea that "likability bias" handicaps women leaders and undermines the effectiveness of groups led by female experts when compared to groups led by male experts (Thomas-Hunt and Phillips, 2004). Men who lead are expected to be and are, in turn, more likable than women who violate what society expects of them when they lead.

ABUSE OF POWER

As director of the National Institute for Environmental Health Sciences and the National Toxicology Program, Dr. Linda Birnbaum was nearly fired for commenting that science should direct policy decisions to prevent cancer. In 2013, Dr. Linda Birnbaum, a toxicologist and microbiologist, likened lax regulation of cancer-causing chemicals to uncontrolled medicines. Environmental exposure to these chemicals caused a "staggering increase in several diseases" like prostate and breast cancers and negatively impacted male reproduction (Birnbaum, 2013). She later said, "I commented that science should be used in policy decision-making. And I was accused of lobbying" (Cornwall, 2019). Her conclusion had caused two Republican Congressmen to complain to her boss, Francis Collins, that "her scientific work has caused discomfort" to industry (Morris and Hamby, 2013). Her editorial "Regulating Toxic Chemicals for Public and Environmental Health" quoted another researcher who said to protect public health, a fundamental toxicology precept that the "dose makes the poison" needed to be upended (Gross and Birnbaum, 2017). Dr. Birnbaum believed that using an approach that accepted one case of cancer per one hundred thousand people was inadequate to protect public health. This approach doesn't result in one case of cancer per one hundred thousand because some people are more vulnerable than others, and other people are exposed daily to mixtures rather than one chemical at a time.

Her words resonated with me. I used the same approach Dr. Birnbaum took when I testified for stricter regulations on "forever chemicals" in New Hampshire. I asserted that the typical risk approach would result in more than one case of cancer per one hundred thousand people since young children and others can be more vulnerable to chemical exposures. Since most regulators were older white men, I outlined how the chemicals impact male reproduction, including reduced penis size (DiNisio et al., 2018), to make a case for more robust protections in drinking water. Such a bold approach may have proved effective in passing stringent protections for drinking water. The state focused on children's effects, which resulted in much more protective drinking water regulation.

Dr. Birnbaum said that after the complaints from Congressmen, the Department of Health and Human Services

(DHHS) leadership didn't give her a raise over two years and, "For the next two years, two and a half years, everything I wrote, every talk I gave, every slide I used, had to be cleared by the Director or someone else that didn't have the background to assess my work" (Cornwall, 2019). But Dr. Birnbaum persevered because she knew she was on the right path. She informed *Science*, "I kept telling myself, as I was feeling bad about being attacked, that if I weren't making a difference, they wouldn't care" (Cornwall, 2019).

While control over the EPA was troubling during the Obama administration, pressure and censorship of science significantly worsened during the Trump administration, according to Dr. Birnbaum, when she was discouraged to speak to the press or completely blocked from doing so without clearance. She added the administration tried to maintain significant control over what she said (Gewin, 2022). Nevertheless, Dr. Birnbaum claimed, "I would say whatever the hell I wanted to during my talk" (Gewin, 2022). She also welcomed reporters to speak with her openly after her talks, when control over her words was harder for her superiors to maintain.

Much freer in retirement, Dr. Birnbaum has generously supported advocacy efforts like mine. She opened herself to interviews for this book and a podcast. She openly shared her concerns with the EPA Pesticides and the Toxics offices. These are the offices that approve pesticides and other chemicals for use. Dr. Birnbaum had raised concerns over the approval and use of several pesticides, including DDT, during her tenure as head of the National Toxicology Program. She said that while the new administration has brought in some good people, the "Old behaviors are still there in the existing staff and some of the long-term employees." As a result, Dr. Birnbaum told me, "I think there needs to be a total house cleaning or moving people to other positions," because "industry would be talking with the EPA regulators and influencing their decision."

HAVE THINGS CHANGED?

In 2015, children poisoned with lead caused by drinking contaminated water in Flint, Michigan, captured national news headlines. At the center of exposing the lead poisoning was Dr. Mona Hanna-Attisha, a pediatrician and professor from Michigan State University.

In her book, *What the Eyes Don't See: A Story of Crisis, Resistance, and Hope in an American City* (Hanna-Attisha, 2018), Dr. Mona (who is commonly referred to by that name) details how her high school friend, a former EPA employee, tipped her off to the "really, really high" lead levels in the Flint water system. Dr. Mona looked at her patients' blood lead levels and found them shockingly high. In September 2015, she revealed that lead levels in children's blood in Flint, Michigan, had doubled after the city changed the drinking water source to the Flint River. Dr. Mona stated, "I did something totally disobedient in the academic doctor world: I literally walked out of my clinic, and I stood up at a press conference and shared this research. Because there was no time, every day that went by was another day that was putting our children at risk" (Fonger, 2020). Dr. Mona felt that "it's our professional obligation to care for the children of Flint (and to tell parents) if we know something" (Fonger, 2020).

The Flint River became the drinking water source to save money since the city was under emergency austerity orders (Krings, Kornberg, and Lane, 2019). However, the water was so bad it caused corrosion in General Motors' (G.M.) car parts, so G.M. made the city switch the water supply back to the Detroit water system (Fonger, 2014a). A G.M. spokesperson said, "We noticed it some time ago (and) the discussions [to revert to Lake Huron water] have been going on for some time" (Fonger, 2014).

Let us pause here for a moment to think. The Flint water was so corrosive "engine crankshafts showed rust after they were machined with river water" (Fonger, 2014b). Yet the state said, "Flint's system is producing safe water, and that chloride levels are considered acceptable—not excellent, which GM requires" (Fonger, 2014). The City of Flint no longer provided corrosion control required by law, so water service lines were corroding, resulting in lead levels up to almost nine hundred times the EPA lead action level in one residence (Del Toral, 2015). Flint residents knew only enough to be skeptical and raise general concerns about the brown water. And then Dr. Mona spoke up. She said it "felt great for about a half an hour after going public [...]. I'm protecting kids. Things are going to change" (Carroll, 2020).

But the pushback was fierce. Like my experience when I exposed the cancer cluster, the response to Dr. Mona from the state agency and government officials gave her "an overwhelming sense of imposter syndrome that maybe I shouldn't have done this. Maybe I should have just kept going about my business as a busy mom, pediatrician, wife. Nothing can prepare you for when the entire state goes after you and tells you you're wrong [...]. When I heard about lead, my life changed," said Dr. Mona (Bock, 2021).

President Obama also didn't help matters. During his May 2016 visit to Flint, he angered many citizens by minimizing the issue at a press conference. Halfway through his speech, he asked for a glass of water and drank it in front of the crowd, followed by statements that while what happened was a moral outrage, it was no longer a medical emergency (Nelson, 2016).

Marc Edwards, a Virginia Tech researcher, who came from Virginia to help with the crisis, was also attacked and dismissed. But the press treated him very differently. Dr. Mona told me that the press asked her, "Who's taking care of your kids? Or who's cooking at home?" Dr. Mona said that Edwards "didn't even live in the state, why [didn't they] ask him who's cooking dinner at home?"

Dr. Mona experienced gender-coded attacks and attempts to undermine her expertise like me, Dr. Bik, and Rachel Carson. Brad Wurfel, from the Michigan Department of Environmental Quality, called her an "unfortunate researcher" and questioned the validity of her data (The Associated Press, 2015). He accused her of "causing near hysteria" when she publicly exposed the high levels of lead in children's blood (The Associated Press, 2015). But Dr. Mona told me she "wore it like a badge of honor since so many amazing women [she] adore[d] had been called the same."

The fallout from the crisis resulted in many people being removed from their positions and criminal charges being brought against some of them. In addition, residents were offered free bottled water for two years under a $450 million state and federal aid package in response to court action and a $626M settlement to cover the costs incurred by Flint residents by the lead-contaminated water (The Associated Press, 2021).

Dr. Mona persevered unphased by the opposition. In 2021, she was awarded $14.4M to collaborate with community leaders, clinical partners, educators, and other stakeholders in Flint to assess and support the health effects in the community (Childhood Lead Poisoning Prevention, 2021). The money set up a registry to track the children exposed to lead-contaminated water (Childhood Lead Poisoning Prevention, 2021). She told me they still must overcome many issues of mistrust, but they have already filled twenty thousand of the one hundred thousand spaces in the registry.

When I spoke with Dr. Mona, she expressed that when she accepts an award, it's "awkward." But she tells herself, "This is not about you; this is about the little brown girl who's watching this and realizing she can do this too." And then she asks herself, "How do we foster more badass girls that are going to do this and not be afraid?"

Ms. Priya Shukla could be an example of one of those little brown girls who is already a "badass" following in Dr. Mona's leadership footsteps. Ms. Shukla characterized herself as a petite, East Indian woman (Shukla and Myhre, 2016). She is a PhD candidate in marine biology at the University of California, Davis. She told me it's challenging for young female scientists coming up through academia: "Academia is a system that was built for privileged white men by privileged white men. White men are in the upper echelons of academia, and they are, in my opinion, deliberately and willfully obtuse about ways in which they are perpetuating the structures that keep others out."

Ms. Shukla has two older white male mentors and a very supportive female professor. However, Ms. Shukla said her thoughts and ideas were ignored during scientific meetings most of the time. She gets frustrated when she feels her voice isn't heard and thinks it's due, at least in part, to her appearance and the fact that she is a young female scientist.

Dr. Elisabeth Bik thought the same thing while working at Stanford. She decided to track how much time men spoke during meetings versus women. She concluded that there was a tendency for men to interrupt women during meetings when they tried to talk (Adamczyk, 2016). Kieran Snyder observed that men interrupted people twice as often as women during meetings in another tech work setting. Also, men were three times as likely to interrupt women as other men (Snyder, 2014). In addition, there were no women in senior positions within the firm who didn't interrupt their male colleagues. "The results suggest that women don't advance in their careers beyond a certain point without learning to interrupt, at least in this male-dominated tech setting" (Snyder, 2014). When senior female leaders are assertive, it feeds the stereotypical gender norms that promote strong female leaders as "bossy, unpleasant, and bitchy" (Snyder, 2014).

However, Ms. Shukla said her female mentor will frequently reiterate what Ms. Shukla noted during the meeting. Then it will be heard and taken seriously. Ms. Shukla said her female mentor recognized her challenges and "helps amplify my voice but always gives me credit." Ms. Shukla thinks it's essential for women to step up and support each other's work. She feels it helps create an efficient and productive work environment for scientific endeavors.

Ms. Shukla also shared that her fieldwork necessitated scientific diving expeditions to collect data and observe oysters. It is unusual for a young female scientist of color to have a scuba diver license (90 percent of the divers are male, and about 70 percent are white) (Zippia, 2022). Ms. Shukla told me that her fieldwork was challenging because she suffered from anxiety exacerbated by scuba diving. But, because she thinks her work is vital, she developed some coping mechanisms to continue collecting her data. For example, she told me that taking a few moments to collect her thoughts when they reached diving depth before starting the work helped control her anxiety.

Ms. Shukla said she noticed a big difference between male- versus female-dominated dive teams. She told me she thought that her anxiety-reducing process irritated the male-dominated teams. She thought male-dominated teams weren't as respectful and patient with her need to collect herself at the bottom before she initiated the tasks. However, when women led the dive team, Ms. Shukla had an entirely different experience. Female-led teams fostered a supportive rapport that made the effort fun and the work more efficient. Overall, she experienced less anxiety with a female-dominated team that took a "more thoughtful and pragmatic approach." Male-dominated teams, she thought, wanted to accomplish tasks with "brute force."

Studies support Ms. Shukla's experience with male-versus female-led scuba teams and found that woman-led teams were collaborative. Although women with expertise are perceived as less likable, gender parity in working groups improved the overall quality and outcomes of the work (Bear and Woolley, 2011; Campbell et al., 2013).

Other studies concluded that gender norms also impact male and female leadership views in the business world. For example, high-potential women who are competent managers often fail the likability test. But competence and likability tend to go hand in hand for similarly accomplished men (Ibarra, Ely, and Kolb, 2013).

It's not only important for female scientists to be active wage-earners, but when there are more female researchers they are more likely to advance understanding of women's health. A recent study found that female scientists are 35 percent more likely to develop medical treatments for women than male-led teams. The study highlights the importance of supporting women and ensuring their active participation in science; however, women represent only 13 percent of patent holders (Senz, 2022). The study also found that everyone benefits from more female scientists, not just women; female scientists are also more likely to study diseases that affect men and women more than male-led teams (Senz, 2022). So, everyone stands to benefit from gender-empowered and inclusive teams.

Teams led by women, however, are not as prevalent as those led by men in academia or industry. One study found that gender bias in faculty members who selected candidates for managerial positions in elite biology, chemistry, and physics labs may be responsible for the paucity of female faculty members (Moss-Racusin et al., 2012). Therefore, "Labs really function as a gateway to the professoriate. So, we think the fact that they're not hiring very many women is important for understanding why there are still so few female faculty members," said Jason Sheltzer, a graduate student in biology at MIT (Trafton, 2014). The study took identical applications for laboratory manager positions and blindly masked them with female- and male-sounding names. Faculty members rated the duplicate applications with female-sounding names as less competent and less hirable than those with the same resume but with a male-sounding name. The faculty members also offered less career mentoring and a lower starting salary to the applications with female-sounding names than males with the same qualifications (Moss-Racusin et al., 2012).

"All of this starts to circle around the idea that despite the fact that many faculty are very well-meaning, subtle stereotypes about who is most likely to succeed can impact the judgment and treatment of individuals," Moss-Racusin noted.

But maybe some faculty are not that well-meaning. In 2015, at the World Conference of Science Journalists in Seoul, South Korea, Professor Tim Hunt, an English biochemist, admitted that he had a reputation for being a chauvinist (Ratcliffe, 2015). He said, "Let me tell you about my trouble with girls [...] three things happen when they are in the lab [...]. You fall in love with them, they fall in love with you, and when you criticize them, they cry" (Ratcliffe, 2015). Dr. Hunt further said he favored single-sex laboratories. Argh.

TIME FOR CHANGE

Since March of 2020, dealing with the challenges of a global pandemic has demonstrated that "the world depends on scientific cooperation to protect us from the threats of new infectious diseases and bioterrorism" (McKeague, 2003). Unfortunately, the distractions caused by gender inequities, political battles, and bias against female scientists described in this book portend more than a little disruption in the future of global cooperation.

Employers can also make some advances, but other improvements require policy changes at the state and federal levels. In February 2022, the passage of the "Ending Forced Arbitration of Sexual Assault and Sexual Harassment Act" was a step in the right direction. The new law makes it illegal for employers to force employees who allege sexual harassment or sexual assault in the workplace to be forced into employer-sponsored mediation. But employees who allege workplace gender discrimination can still be compelled to arbitrate their cases (Gerstein, 2022).

We must continue to understand and talk about the bias and overcome gender stereotypes to encourage young women to enter the science field. While we have taken some necessary steps forward, we have not made sufficient progress in normalizing women in leadership positions in the science field so they can lead by example.

CHAPTER 8

BUILDING THE BENCH

—

"Leaders don't set out to climb the ladder.
They rise by lifting others up."

—JO MILLER, AUTHOR AND GLOBALLY RENOWNED
AUTHORITY ON WOMEN'S LEADERSHIP

My father tried to pick up my frame pack and stopped due to its heft.

"What do you have in this thing? Rocks?" (Actually, there were a lot of rocks in my pack).

I returned from a summer of hiking and mapping geology in dusty and hot South Dakota, Wyoming, and Montana at a geologic field camp. It had been one of the best summers of my life. I learned so much, saw so much, and made new friends. I brought some "souvenirs" home with me. They weren't T-shirts or postcards but unique rocks I had picked up during the trip.

Ever since I was a young girl, I had collected rocks on family trips. Then I researched and tried to identify them. I had an excellent rock collection for the school science class competition in fifth grade. So awesome that someone stole it.

My mother fostered my interest in science from a young age. She took me on trips to nature and science museums, and she organized projects for us to do together all the time, like making sand sculptures and plant terrariums. We also took trips that were not typical for families with young children. Those to Death Valley, Joshua Tree Forest, and La Brea Tar Pits were more memorable trips.

When I was a high school senior, I was unsure what major to pursue in college. My computer programming course teacher was impressed enough with my class projects that he told me I should major in computer science in college. So, at his suggestion, the following fall I started as a computer science major at Syracuse University. But I quickly realized computer science was not for me. During a conversation with my mother, she suggested I try geology or anthropology since I loved to collect rocks.

The next semester I took both courses. My mother was right, I loved geology, so I changed my major. In college, many great professors encouraged me. Before graduation, Dr. Dickey, the dean of the Earth Science program, handed me a rock hammer as a gift. He asked me what colleges I was looking at for graduate school. He said, "An hour from the mountains, an hour from Boston, near the seacoast, go to the University of New Hampshire." Following his advice, I applied for and was accepted into the graduate program at the University of New Hampshire and headed off to Durham.

Sheri[8] told me she was beginning her junior undergraduate year at a prominent university at around the same time. Her father was an engineer, and her mom was a piano teacher. She said that her father recognized her math and science skills and encouraged her to pursue a career in engineering. When Sheri started college, she majored in civil engineering and earned excellent grades in all the classes required for first- and second-year civil engineering students. As a junior, she had to choose to focus on structural or environmental engineering. "Most women selected environmental engineering, and most male students selected structural engineering," Sheri told me. But, she said, "I was very interested in both." Her university had a tremendous structural engineering program. "I told my advisor that I was considering structural engineering and then going to architecture school after that." Sheri said her advisor told her architecture "would not be as welcoming for her." He added, "You might want to reconsider. Architecture is just not a profession that females choose." She said she might not have decided to pursue an architecture program eventually, but "that was the first time I was ever told, because of my gender, I should reconsider my academic path."

Sheri said she thought her advisor was "trying to provide [her] with good advice" and that she felt he was just being honest with her. "I think he was looking out for me. But the message speaks for itself. Looking back, now I see." In the

---

8   A pseudonym, as she requested that I not use her real name.

end, Sheri chose the environmental engineering path suggested by her advisor. But, if I had been her advisor, I would have told Sheri to pursue her passion regardless of the gender bias of the other students or faculty members.

As for Sheri, mentor bias may have a profound intentional or unintentional effect on academic choices for young women. Sheri and I and many other female scientists I interviewed benefitted from organic mentoring relationships (i.e., parents and teachers) that encouraged us to explore scientific disciplines.

However, we must train teachers and mentors to abandon gender stereotypes that deter young women from entering STEM fields and cause them to leave the field. "Gender-stereotypical beliefs should be tackled among teachers and other gatekeepers who are potentially involved in the development of vocational interests among children and secondary students" (Makarova, Aeschlimann, and Herzog, 2019). We must improve girls' participation in STEM education so they have equal access to traditionally male-dominated "green" jobs, enabling them to contribute to an equitable, just transition (Jeffs, 2022).

Q: WHEN SHOULD WE START ENCOURAGING YOUNG WOMEN TO PURSUE SCIENCE AS A CAREER PATH?

A: START EARLY!

An interesting study concluded that it is essential to address gender stereotypes early in a child's life. When surveyed, boys and girls at age five are equally likely to think their gender can be brilliant. But by the time girls are six to seven years old, they are less likely than boys to judge other girls as competent and capable (Khan, 2017). Lin Bian, a graduate student in psychology at the University of Illinois at Urbana-Champaign and author of the study, stated, "We really need to know when this problematic stereotype first emerges [so] we know when to intervene to avoid these negative consequences on girls' educational decisions and their future career choices" (Khan, 2017) because these inaccurate perceptions persist later in life. Another study documented the persistence of these early perceptions of gender competency. The study found that men in college-level STEM classes overestimated the capabilities of male students. At the same time, they consistently underestimated the abilities of female STEM students (Grunspan et al., 2016). This phenomenon is more pronounced when the subject matter is perceived to be more masculine, like chemistry, math, and physics (Makarova, Aeschlimann, and Herzog, 2019).

Girls often think their ability in math and science is lower than their actual ability (self-efficacy); this factor can play a factor in academic and career aspirations as early as fifteen years of age (Makarova, Aeschlimann, and Herzog, 2019). Dr. Kristen Lindquist, an associate professor of psychology and neuroscience at the University of North Carolina at Chapel Hill, stated, "As a young woman, there are lots of signs out there that this isn't for you, as you progress, and there's lots of imposter syndrome and lots of uncertainty" (Huckins, 2021). Dr. Lindquist also noted that it's helpful to have someone keep saying to you, "You can do this, and I know you're smart; and let me show you the way." She further noted that mentors can help instill self-confidence and encourage involvement, leading to retention in STEM fields.

Hopefully, enrollment and retention in STEM fields have improved over the few years. But indicators say otherwise. As of 2017, based on "the occupational aspirations of fifteen-year-old adolescents, the prognosis for change in gender-based disparities in occupational and academic choices suggests that gender segregation in the education and labor market will remain persistent" (Makarova, Aeschlimann, and Herzog, 2019).

MENTORS HELP WOMEN SEE THEMSELVES AS SUCCESSFUL IN STEM ROLES

Shanika Amarakoon, a young female immigrant from Sri Lanka, whom I met while campaigning for office, is an example of why it is crucial to young female scientists of color for schools to promote diversity in academic faculty.

Ms. Amarakoon told me her father was a professor who originally came to the United States on a student visa. Ms. Amarakoon grew up in the United States in a predominantly white rural community. After many years, her family finally achieved US citizenship just before Ms. Amarakoon turned eighteen.

The culture for women in Sri Lanka, in some ways, is very progressive for women; they had had female presidents and prime ministers for a long time, the latter since 1960, when Sirimavo Bandaranaike was the first elected female prime minister. Ms. Amarakoon said women "were encouraged to become doctors or scientists or lawyers or engineers" and are highly respected.

But when she went to school in the United States, Ms. Amarakoon said she pushed away her culture to fit in with the other kids. She told me that when she got to college, her fellow students in engineering school were "mostly young white males from wealthy, conservative families." As a young woman of color, Ms. Amarakoon told me she didn't feel like she belonged. In addition, she said she didn't feel connected with faculty members. Because she thought she didn't belong, Ms. Amarakoon said she considered dropping out of engineering early in her undergraduate years. Instead, she decided to speak with the associate dean and professor of civil and environmental engineering, Terri Norton, who uses the nickname "Trudy." Trudy has a bachelor's and master's degree and a PhD in civil engineering. When Ms. Amarakoon told Trudy she didn't feel connected and was considering dropping out, Trudy told her, "No, I think you need to stick with us." Ms. Amarakoon's conversation with Trudy made a big difference, and she stayed with the undergraduate civil engineering program. Ms. Amarakoon went on to graduate school for environmental management, and now she works for an environmental advocacy organization.

In Ms. Amarakoon's case, she envisioned success in STEM through Trudy. So, when Ms. Amarakoon questioned her ability to be successful, she was able to see herself in Trudy's position, and it was easier to imagine a future path in civil engineering.

Mathematica Senior Fellow Dr. Catherine McLaughlin said mentees envision their success when they relate to someone they want "to emulate, professionally or otherwise" (McLaughlin, 2010). Dr. Audrey Murrell, a professor at the University of Pittsburgh, agrees. She said mentorship helped young women feel a sense of inclusion and self-confidence. "Mentoring is not just about opening the door. It's about making people feel welcome. It's about developing them; it's about providing for the whole person" (Huckins, 2021).

DOES GENDER-MATCHING MATTER FOR MENTEES?

Female mentees tend to have a strong preference for female mentors or advisors. Mentees often prefer someone they look up to as successful or see as representing themselves. But the evidence on the effectiveness of matched versus unmatched gender mentoring is conflicting. One recent study found that mentees consider gender-matching essential, but there was no measurable effect on academic outcomes with gender-matching (Blake-Beard et al., 2011). Other studies have found that same-gender mentorship is crucial during the first two years of college when most women consider leaving STEM programs. Female mentors helped young women pursue engineering careers by creating a sense of belonging and improved self-confidence, leading to success and retention in engineering (Dennehy and Dasgupta, 2017).

Sheri told me she wished her male mentor did not raise the issue of gender disparity to discourage her from following her interest in architecture. Instead, like I would have, she felt her mentor should have focused on academics and encouraged her to follow her passion for architecture regardless of gender.

But, Dr. Linda Birnbaum, the former director of the National Institute for Environmental Health Sciences, shared with me that "It's really important to establish a robust network of support [...]. I had some very, very supportive male mentors." Her network included men, not just women; the right male mentor was very supportive. She added it was essential to have a variety of mentors throughout scientific careers. It is beneficial to incorporate male perspectives for career development, and male mentors can help female scientists develop strategies for navigating challenging issues.

Dr. Birnbaum, who retired in 2019, recalled how it was challenging to be a woman in a predominantly male field, and having male and female mentors might have helped. She stated, "When I was young, especially, it was hard to establish networks," and shared that, "The guys would all want to get together in the bar. And that just wasn't a place that I was going to go get together with them." Dr. Birnbaum also shared that during meetings, "One guy would follow another guy into the men's room, if they were having a discussion, obviously I wasn't going to do that." She added that it was harder to navigate this situation, often leaving her feeling like an outsider. When Dr. Birnbaum shared challenges balancing work and family life during her first year of teaching with the female dean of her department, she felt unsupported. Her dean told her she "had a husband who could support her, who could put a roof over her head and food on the table for her and her children, so she should stop worrying about her career."

Dr. Birnbaum's stories remind me of my time as an environmental consultant. Male clients and company executives often would not include me in subcontractor get-togethers or client meetings. It was easy to feel like an outsider; it made it especially hard to advance my standing in the organization. Perhaps the situation would have been different if women held higher positions within the organization and could mentor and support younger women like me in improving our status within the organization.

FEMALE MENTORS CAN BE MORE LIKELY TO SUPPORT CAREER PROGRESSION

Mentors can also help junior female scientists gain recognition for their work and help them publish since publication in scientific journals is commonly a measure of career progression and success. One study found that only 30 percent of published authors were female (Ouyang, Harrington, and Rodriguez, 2019); 36 percent of the primary authors and 26 percent of the senior authors in the sample were females (Reardon, 2021; Chatterjee and Werner, 2021). Between 1994 and 2014, publications with women as first authors in six high-impact medical journals increased, but they have plateaued or declined (Filardo et al., 2016). Another study found that the overall proportion of published studies with females listed as first authors increased between 1989 and 2009 in three pharmaceutical journals. However, while studies with females listed as last authors increased between 1989 and 1999, Dotson concluded that a gender disparity still exists (Dotson, 2011). But Ouyang, Harrington, and Rodriguez (2019) concluded that "When women served as the corresponding author, they published manuscripts with more female last authors, are more likely to have female coauthors, and had more female authors."

Female scientists are also less cited in scientific journals than men. "Undercited scholarship affects who gets hired, tenured, funded, published, and promoted. Undercited scholarship trivializes the contributions of women and marginalized groups, making disciplines appear whiter and more male" (12 Women Scholars, 2021). Dr. Reshma Jagsi, a radiation oncologist and bioethicist at the University of Michigan in Ann Arbor, said although publishing in scientific journals is considered a measure of career progression, "It shows just how much impact unconscious biases can have" (Reardon, 2021).

MENTORS CAN HELP NAVIGATE "UNFRIENDLY" ENVIRONMENTS

While the ultimate goal is to dismantle environments that are not supportive for women, realistically, women will need to navigate these environments until that goal is met. Mentors can help female scientists feel included despite the negativity surrounding them. I benefited from a male mentor, Andy, who was very supportive while managing a particularly challenging client. In the end, I successfully managed the client, who followed me for twenty-five years when I took new jobs.

Also, as a freshman Democratic legislator elected during a Republican trifecta, I could have faced an unfriendly environment in the New Hampshire House of Representatives. But I was lucky to have met Renny Cushing, a veteran male legislator, through my advocacy work on the Governor's Pediatric Cancer Task Force. When I was first elected, he helped me write bills and get them through the legislature. Then I watched how he organized and formed coalitions to support legislation and got others involved to help push back on regulators about important issues in my community. I also sought advice and support from Senator Dan Feltes, a young leader in the New Hampshire Senate. I learned how to testify. I realized it was essential to support other legislators and how to do it—how to show support for others' legislation, how to use what I learned to help others, how to push levers to make things happen. The mentorship and support of these men facilitated establishing crucial public health protections for my community and the entire state. Now, I use the skills I learned to help others and continue to write policy proposals for others and help get them passed.

Dr. Judith Walters, the senior investigator in the Neurophysiological Pharmacology section at the National Institutes for Health (NIH), attributed her early career successes to having good mentors at critical times in her career. When she came to NIH, she recalled that Thomas Chase ran a lab and "was very well connected; he helped me go to meetings and get to know people." Dr. Walters also recalled two other male mentors who were instrumental in her success, but she also encountered other men who were not. For example, when she applied for a PhD program, she was asked, "Why do you want to get a PhD? You're a woman." Another highly respected male faculty member asked, "Who let her in?" when she entered a meeting (Scheinert, 2015).

WHAT'S IN IT FOR THEM (THE MENTORS)?

Dr. Birnbaum shared that she felt a responsibility to mentor young women. She said that as a young scientist, she had encountered other women "Who had achieved a certain degree of success, but they weren't trying to help other people." She said, "I'll never forget it. I went to see a woman speak. Her name was Rosalyn Yarrow, and she was a Nobel Laureate." After her talk, Dr. Birnbaum shared that she went to meet her, and when she tried to talk to her, "She wouldn't give me the time of day. I remember that was kind of discouraging." Her experience with Dr. Yarrow and others helped Dr. Birnbaum develop a sense of responsibility to help female scientists. She said, "It's important to return the favor by mentoring other people."

Mathematica Senior Fellow Dr. Catherine McLaughlin said, "Mentoring should be a more formal requirement that is lauded." She said we must "Rethink what it means to contribute to the field" (McLaughlin, 2010).

WHO ARE THE BEST MENTORS?

Parents can create stimulating and supportive environments that form interests and provide experiences that foster young women's self-confidence (Schwartz, Lowe, and Rhodes, 2012). And as the research shows that early experiences impact later occupational choices of women as adults, it makes sense that parents can be important mentors for young women (Roberts, 1992; Khan, 2017).

Bonnie Bracey Sutton, a STEM educator appointed to the National Information Infrastructure Advisory Council by President Bill Clinton, told me in her experience, communicating with parents, especially moms, made a huge difference. As a science teacher in a racially diverse community, she enlisted help from moms, overcame challenges with less than supportive administrators, and connected with girls on STEM topics. Ms. Sutton told me that when she covered topics with community relevance like water quality using hands-on lessons, the kids and their parents were excited to learn about issues that directly impacted their lives. Ms. Sutton told me some of the mothers who helped her organize school science trips became environmental leaders in the community; one opened a school. She also said that most of her female students followed a path into science and became either physicians, teachers, or environmentalists. A few of her students became school administrators who focused on school science education. Mentorship can also come from community programs and school-based or youth programs (Schwartz, Lowe, and Rhodes, 2012).

Depending on the situation and the mentee, both formal and informal mentoring relationships can be helpful for women's long-term development as scientists. For example, Ms. Amarakoon reached out to Trudy for advice and formed an informal mentorship. Informal mentors develop independently, often providing a sounding board for advice and an avenue for shared experiences when faced with challenges in academic or other professional environments (McLaughlin, 2010). In Ms. Amarakoon's situation, an informal mentoring relationship worked.

However, developing formal mentoring programs that include mentor training and support in schools, academia, and community settings are likely to benefit the community and encourage young women to develop an interest in the sciences. Formal mentoring is an assigned relationship usually structured with goals, schedules, training, and evaluation. Formal mentor relationships could be either within the mentee's discipline or outside and are more like a coach than a friend who advises on careers and goals (McLaughlin, 2010). It's essential to provide training and reinforce the importance of mentoring by formalizing it as a primary responsibility of professionals. For example, Dr. Jen Heemstra, a chemist at Emory University in Atlanta, Georgia, said when you get an academic job, "All of a sudden, you are a mentor, but there's very few places or opportunities where you actually get formal training in how to mentor. So, I think that alone is one of the biggest challenges, is just this process of then realizing that there's the skill set that you haven't really, you often haven't, had a chance to purposely build" (Gould, 2021). Dr. Heemstra views mentoring as a "role [that] is a bit like an athletic coach. I want to help everyone be able to perform at their best. And different people have different modes of motivation" (Gould, 2021).

The pandemic has challenged mentoring relationships and work environments, especially for female scientists with families and where parenting and caregiver responsibilities rest disproportionately on women. Mentoring relationships were likely disrupted at the start of the pandemic because so much relied on developing a personal connection, which is more difficult via Zoom or conference calls. "Not being able to physically meet with the people in your research group can be really difficult," said Vidita Viyada, a professor of neurobiology at the Tata Institute for Fundamental Research in Mumbai, India (Gould, 2021).

But the silver lining of the pandemic could be that it pushed organizations to make Zoom webinars and meetings commonplace so that, in some ways, networking and meeting other scientists around the globe has been more accessible. With remote access, hopping on a thirty- or sixty-minute professional meeting is much easier for a busy parent than finding a sitter, getting in the car, or traveling by plane to participate. While there are some drawbacks to not meeting face-to-face, the silver lining is that more scientists are willing to collaborate by jumping on a Zoom or Microsoft Teams meeting. In addition, holding online meetings reduces travel and fossil fuel consumption, which is better for the planet overall. Maintaining mentoring networks is especially important for science moms already challenged to meet the demands of career and family life.

CHAPTER 9

SCIENCE MOMS

—

*"When the whole world hates you at work
or ignores you, a child will enrich your life
with unconditional love."*

—UNKNOWN MIT NOBEL LAUREATE (MONOSSON, 2008).

"You can't work with a baby in the house. There's no way," my partner said.

My business partner's response to my becoming a mother who worked was shockingly sexist.

To get to this point in my career and life, I had finished my undergraduate degree, attended graduate school, and worked in consulting for almost nine years. Before this, when we decided my husband would take a new job in the Chicago area, I started to work at a national consulting firm in downtown Chicago. When my husband surprised me by saying that we would move back to the Northeast, I was thrilled. My employer transferred my position to Massachusetts, and my clients followed me. I advanced to a management position in the consulting firm and added a handful more private and defense-industry clients.

When my colleague and friend convinced me to leave my corporate job and start a company, I thought it would be perfect. We talked many times, sharing our desires to start our respective families. I would work out of my house, hire a nanny, and be around for my child. Since my husband traveled extensively on business, one of us had to be around. So, I left my job with a national consulting firm to start a consulting business. Most of my clients followed me to my new firm.

In my new position, I worked until the day before I gave birth to my first son and couldn't take much time off after he was born. He napped in a bassinet on my desk, and we breastfed while I wrote reports, managed projects, and participated in conference calls. When he got a little older, a hired nanny assisted with other childcare duties while I worked in the house. I wanted to be successful both as a mom and a small business owner. However, I realize we were privileged to have an in-home nanny, something not everyone can accomplish.

But the friendship and business partnership started falling apart soon after my colleague and I started our company. My partner tried to diminish my client billings and future bookings, thereby undermining my standing in the organization, when he tried to hire additional male partners. Later, he admitted he had been wrong. In the end, the issues with my early business partner were probably for the best, as they gave me the courage and motivation to start my own business when my son was six months old.

I wholeheartedly agree with Anne G. Rosenwald's statement that "Nevertheless, most of the women [...] confirm that being a scientist is something they wouldn't change, despite the pains necessary to achieve a balance" (Rosenwald, 2011). To break the cycle of women leaving the workforce to start a family, we must model women in leadership for boys from a young age to arrest gender stereotypes like my partner's. I always thought it essential for my sons to see me as both a mom and a working scientist.

WHEN IS THE BEST TIME FOR FEMALE SCIENTISTS TO START A FAMILY?

I had waited until I was thirty-five years old to start a family. Like many female scientists, my career had taken top billing when my academic pursuit and career path were prioritized over starting a family. I wasn't alone; many other female scientists chose to delay motherhood so their academic or career pursuits did not suffer.

Dr. Linda Birnbaum, the former director of the National Institute for Environmental Health Sciences, shared that female graduate students "always want to know when the best time is to have a baby. I tell them, there's never a good or better time; you'll adjust. You'll work with whatever you get. If what you want to do is have children, when you're trying to get established is the time your biological clock is ticking."

One of my mentors from my master's degree program at Georgetown University, Dr. Nawar Shara, the director of the Department of Biostatistics and Bioinformatics at MedStar Health Research Institute (MHRI), said she planned to start a family after completing her PhD at American University. She got pregnant about six months into her marriage. She told me, at first, she thought it was going to be an obstacle for her to complete her PhD, but she didn't dwell on it because life brings so many things one can't control. She told me, "There's going to be lots of tragedies, sickness, death, accidents, lots of things, and if each one of those will chip a certain part of you, and it will keep you wounded for a little bit, but that one should make you stronger and more determined to make a difference in your life and others."

Women cited high childcare costs, housing costs, and opportunity costs as factors contributing to delayed motherhood (Tavernise et al., 2021). Birth control is used to delay starting a family to maintain control of their economic situation and career path. However, for the last several years, the government has aggressively chipped away at female reproductive health care, and, consequently, women still do not have equal rights to plan their families. Women must be empowered with greater personhood equality and possess greater agency and autonomy to plan their families with improved access to free or affordable reproductive health care, childcare, early education assistance, and universal and family medical leave (Potter et al., 2019).

As more women of all social classes prioritized education and employment over the last decade, the decline in population growth since the 1930s steepened; pregnancy rates fell 28 percent for women in their twenties over the previous decade (Tavernise et al., 2021). The rate of unwanted pregnancies declined in the ten years before the pandemic (Jones, Witwer, and Jerman, 2019). According to a 2021 study, Amanda Jean Stevenson, a demographer at the University of Colorado, stated that "One of the big shifts has been fewer people having kids before they wanted to" (Tavernise et al., 2021). However, disruptions in access to reproductive health care during the COVID-19 pandemic may have interrupted the previous decreasing trend of unplanned pregnancies (Almeda, 2021).

As they delayed motherhood, over the last ten years, the rate of women in their twenties graduating with college degrees increased faster than their male counterparts, suggesting that women delayed childbearing to pursue academic goals (Tavernise et al., 2021). Dr. Monica Malta, an epidemiologist at the University of Toronto, decided to delay parenthood until she approached forty. It didn't seem like the right time in her career progression until then. She wanted to start a family once she was more secure but instead decided not to apply for a tenure-track job and took a leave of absence to start in vitro fertilization. She said, "I think it's very common for most women in STEM to wait [...] because our training takes a lot of time," and noted that many of her friends chose work over having children (Heidt, 2021).

OVER THE LAST TEN YEARS, WOMEN ARE INCREASINGLY DECIDING TO BREAK THE GLASS CEILING BEFORE CLIMBING THE "MATERNAL WALL."

According to Merriam Webster's dictionary, the glass ceiling is a term first used in 1984 for an "intangible barrier that prevents women and minorities from obtaining upper-level positions." In the 1980s and '90s, one rarely saw female scientists in high academic and corporate positions. While progress has been made, as of 2017 to 2018, women still only occupy 44 percent of the tenure-track positions and 36 percent of the full professorship positions at universities (AAUW, 2022). In addition, in 2019, only twenty-four women led biotech firms (Dunn, 2019) and women held only 26 percent of the 155 government laboratory science, technology, engineering, and math (STEM) leadership roles (Russell and Metcalf, 2019).

Female scientists had to overcome social biases and persistent cultural beliefs that undermined their ability to advance, chiefly that women should stay home with their kids (Ferrante, 2019) or that men are a family's breadwinners. I was shocked when faced with my business partner's assertion that I could not do both, successfully continuing my professional career and having children. Dr. Isabel Escobar, a chemical engineering professor at the University of Kentucky, had a similar experience when she adopted a new baby between university positions. When she arrived at her new workplace, her new colleagues had only known her as a mom, where at her previous position she had developed a track record as a professional without children. Dr. Escobar noted, "Her new job, with new colleagues, came with biases she hadn't previously encountered" (Ogden, 2019).

Unfortunately, it's not uncommon for very successful women suddenly to find their proficiency questioned once they become pregnant, take maternity leave, or adopt flexible work schedules. "Their performance evaluations may plummet, and their political support evaporates," said Dr. Joan C. Williams, a law professor (Williams, 2004). Dr. Escobar "struggled to figure out how to get her colleagues, especially men, to realize that she is fully capable of performing her job and being a mom at the same time" (Ogden, 2019). Dr. Escobar noted that "Dealing with bias against working mothers is something that 'no one prepares you for'" (Ogden, 2019).

WHEN PREGNANT, SOME FEMALE SCIENTISTS FACE UNIQUE WORKPLACE CHALLENGES.

For some female scientists, the nature of their work may pose a safety risk. Precautions during pregnancy are critical since chemical exposures can harm early fetal development. An example of detrimental prenatal exposure is Bucky Bailey, whose mother worked in a DuPont laboratory in West Parkersburg, VA. Bucky was born with facial deformities thought to be related to his mother's exposure to "forever chemicals" or PFAS while working in DuPont's laboratory (Mordock, 2016). "The first trimester of pregnancy—before many women feel comfortable disclosing their pregnancy—can be the most vulnerable time" (Kuehn, 2019). Some institutions have policies to protect pregnant female scientists. Some created manuals that itemize potential work hazards, including exposure to chemicals or solvents, lifting, and other hazards, over and above federal Title IX workplace protections for pregnant students, faculty, and staff (The Pregnant Scholar, 2021). The Pregnancy Discrimination Act also seeks to protect pregnant workers from discrimination (U.S. Equal Employment Opportunity Commission, 2022).

As a small business owner, I wore all hats and, from time to time, had to work on hazardous sites. But I hired contractors to help cover field site work during the first trimester of my two pregnancies. When my first son was born, at times, I had to juggle fieldwork and pumping breastmilk to ensure he had an ample supply while I was away. And his allergies required me to continue breastfeeding for an extended time, just another adjustment to be negotiated, not a career-ending crisis.

Fortunately, most institutions have policies to support pregnant researchers, but these policies should be universal. Institutional and employment policies can include paid family leave and laboratory safety precautions. "People come up with all kinds of creative solutions," said Dr. Shubha Tole, senior professor at the Tata Institute of Fundamental Research in Mumbai, India (Kuehn, 2019). For example, when Dr. Jillian Nissen found the smell in the animal lab nauseating during her first trimester while working as a researcher at State University at Stony Brook, laboratory staff assisted her. She was able to limit her time in that area. "Having a really good supportive" project advisor "and a group of peers helped with those challenges," she said (Kuehn, 2019). "There were some chemicals that we were using in the labs that I had to be a lot more cautious around," explained Dr. Nissen, who consulted her physician and did research on her own. "I got a lot more careful about masks and gloves with certain things that I normally wouldn't have worried about" (Kuehn, 2019).

Some women can successfully schedule, or at least intend to plan, their pregnancies around academic or other career milestones. For example, Dr. Marla McIntosh stated she timed the birth of her first child for the summer directly after her (successful) tenure review. As a result, she "didn't miss a single class" in her new position (Monosson, 2008).

Like Dr. McIntosh, Dr. Birnbaum was concerned about her pregnancy's impact on receiving tenure at the National Institutes of Health (NIH) and hid her third pregnancy. "So, I dressed very carefully" to go before the committee that would hear her application for tenure. Dr. Birnbaum thought her pursuit for tenure would not be successful if the committee knew she was pregnant. She told me, "And the day after I was told I made tenure, I went to my boss and told him I've got to take the summer off. And he looked at me like I was crazy."

MOTHERHOOD CHANGES EVERYTHING

"In our case, the arrival of children was equivalent to an earthquake or tsunami. It drastically changed our outlook on life, our rhythms, and our interests," said Dr. Avivia Brecher (Monosson, 2008). I would supplement this statement with "in a good way." Female scientists face conflicting social pressures when deciding whether to work or work after having children. For me, while it was challenging when my sons were little, I could not imagine my life without them. At times, I felt guilty that I wasn't spending all my time with my kids.

Dr. Shara told me she never felt guilty about continuing to work. She had her second child while she was finishing her PhD dissertation. Now she has four children, and she never stopped working. But Dr. Shara's sister came from Syria to live with her when her first child was born for almost four years. Then, her cousin, who had just retired from her job, for nearly seven years spent days and evenings with Dr. Shara's children. Although she always wanted to have seven children but stopped at four, Dr. Shara told me she has much respect for colleagues who chose not to have any children because "the minute you decide to have kids, everything changes in life."

Dr. Birnbaum shared similar feelings of conflict about having children at a young age and a career. She said, at the time, even her father didn't understand her desire to return to the lab rather than stay home with her first child. Dr. Birnbaum continued to work and eventually became director of one of twenty-seven research institutes and centers that comprise the NIH.

"I have frequently been questioned, especially by women, of how I could reconcile family life with a scientific career. Well, it has not been easy."

—MARIE CURIE, TWO-TIME NOBEL PRIZE
WINNER AND MOTHER OF IRENE-JOLIOT-
CURIE, WHO ALSO WON THE NOBEL PRIZE

Many female scientists leave work to have children or, like Dr. Shara, never enter tenure-track positions. Dr. Nanette Pazdernik, a cellular biologist, affiliated with Washington University School of Medicine, St. Louis, Missouri, said her husband completely agreed with her decision to stay home with their first child because her pay as a PhD researcher was so low, "[they] didn't need my [her] pittance of a salary" (Monosson, 2008).

Dr. Judith Walters, the senior investigator in the Neurophysiological Pharmacology section at NIH, said as a young principal investigator (PI), she faced "strong social disapproval for going back to work when her children were young" (Scheinert, 2015). Likewise, biologist Dr. Aarathi Prasad's boss said that she didn't work as hard as expected after giving birth and that having a family was her "fault" (Sharma, 2014).

MOTHERHOOD CAN RESULT IN ECONOMIC PENALTIES FOR FEMALE SCIENTISTS

Over the last several years, women have made no progress in narrowing the gender pay gap; women earned 84 percent of men's hourly wage in 2020 (Barroso and Brown, 2021). In addition, the pay gap widened for older women who made trade-offs for caregiving responsibilities. For example, women took part-time jobs or more flexible work schedules, resulting in lower pay (Barroso and Brown, 2021). As a result, women had less market experience than their male counterparts, resulting in reduced wages and a lack of career advancement (Madowitz, Rowell, and Hamm, 2016).

Since 2014, women graduating with four or more years of college have outpaced men, reaching a peak of 38.3 percent of women completing four-year degrees in 2020 (Statista, 2021).

Still, between 2017 and 2018, women were paid less than men at every faculty rank (AAUW, 2022).

Employers discriminated against mothers but rewarded fathers (Correll, Benard, and Paik, 2007). When similarly aged men become fathers, they are viewed as more responsible and more favorably as workers, while women experience a penalty as mothers (Elliott, 2017). A study in 2017 concluded that, overall, fathers incur an average wage increase of more than 6 percent with each child, while women experience, on average, a 4 percent decrease in salary per child. For men, employers consider fatherhood a "valued characteristic, signaling perhaps a greater work commitment, stability, and deservingness," said Michelle Budig, Sociology Department Chair at the University of Massachusetts, Amherst.

On the other hand, employers often perceive mothers as less productive, "exhausted, and distracted at work" (Budig, 2014). Another survey found that men seen as caregivers boosted their reputations. Still, women with children were viewed as less competent, penalized with lower starting salaries, and considered less committed than women without children (Correll, Benard, and Paik, 2007). Employers just assume science moms are "no longer ambitious [...]. You just want an easier, more flexible job," Dr. Torres claimed (Heidt, 2021). Dr. Mary Ann Mason was a "gender equity trailblazer" and the first female dean at the University of California at Berkeley. She said the science field is very competitive, and "although they didn't always say it outright, most male scientists were not eager to take on women because they didn't think they would be 100 percent focused on projects" (Kuehn, 2019).

WHAT CAUSES FEMALE SCIENTIST MOMS
TO LEAVE SCIENCE?

Women often cite difficulty balancing work and family responsibilities as a reason for leaving the workforce. But relatively little research has specifically explored why women quit engineering and computing fields and how it could be ameliorated (Corbett and Hill, 2015). One of the few surveys of nearly nine thousand people from 128 countries conducted in 2020 found that more than one-third (34 percent) of mothers in full-time careers in STEM had left those positions after their first child (Powell, 2021). Another study showed the drop-off rate might be as high as 43 percent (Cech and Blair-Loy, 2019).

The drop-off rate after the firstborn is likely due to struggling to make it all work, with little professional return for all the efforts. Even when the stated goals are to support diversity, unrecognized or intentional micro-aggressions in academic or industry workplaces can make women feel ostracized and lead to dropout (Hall, Schmader, and Croft, 2015). Dr. Torres said, "Mothers can't do it all because they are already doing a lot more. Then, when a mom chooses to leave work or to work part-time, it looks like a personal decision." She offers that scientist fathers rarely face a choice between working full-time or part-time due to family responsibilities (Powell, 2021). Dr. Kasturi Datta, biotechnology professor in the School of Environmental Sciences in Delhi, India, said, "Though there are a lot of women scientists out there, many get lost in their careers. We have to prevent the loss of young talent and attract young women scientists to at least continue their research" (Sharma, 2014).

The opportunity cost for scientist mothers leaving the workplace or taking less-demanding jobs while balancing new parenting challenges is high but often not tallied. A 2015 survey found that 62 percent of working mothers and 36 percent of working fathers said they switched to a less-demanding job or stopped working altogether to care for children (Paquette and Craighill, 2015). When women adjust their schedules for childcare, the long-term costs are much larger than just salary loss. They include forgoing contributions to retirement savings and social security benefits and flattening wage-growth trajectory. One study found that women can lose between "two and four times their annual salary when they leave the workforce" to cover caregiving responsibilities (Madowitz, Rowell, and Hamm, 2016).

In recent decades, the United States, once a leader, has fallen behind other countries in the number of women who participate in the workforce. In 2010, it was ranked seventeenth among twenty-two industrialized countries: a fall from sixth place in 1990 (Madowitz, Rowell, and Hamm, 2016). According to the Center for American Progress, about one-third of the United States' reduced ranking was attributed to family-friendly policies in other countries, including government-supplemented childcare dollars and paid family leave policies, which enable parents and caregivers to address caregiving struggles (Madowitz, Rowell, and Hamm, 2016).

The United States is falling behind other countries that support women who wish to have a family and a career. We need family-friendly initiatives to support women in the workforce and maintain a strong economy founded on a thriving middle class. This may seem costly, but the costs for inaction are far higher, especially as female scientists mature.

CHAPTER 10

SEX PLUS AGE AND WISDOM

—

*"There is no greater power in the world than
the zest of a post-menopausal woman."*

—MARGARET MEAD

I stood before the packed room of about two hundred and fifty people with my notecards in my hand. It was an awful time for a hot flash. *Not now*, I thought to myself. I recalled that my mom called them "power surges." Thinking about how people try to turn this inopportune discomfort into female empowerment annoyed me. It didn't make me feel powerful—just distracted and uncomfortable.

It was another evening campaign forum in the 2018 Democratic Primary for New Hampshire's 1st US Congressional District race. Again, I had to convince the room full of voters that my passion for protecting science and addressing climate change was worthy of their vote. Speaking to a large group like this—convincing them to vote for me—was entirely different than presenting data to a room full of engineers or defense industry manufacturers. During my career, I had been a scientist sitting in front of my computer analyzing data and writing reports or out in the field organizing field teams and inspecting properties for environmental issues. I never thought I would do something like this, and I wasn't sure how to convince them to vote for me.

I looked from face to face in the crowd and wondered if anyone could see how red my face was. Surely it must be obvious. Or could people see the sweat that formed on my brow even though it was a cold night in February in northern New Hampshire?

As a state legislator and member of a community that faced environmental pollution, I had learned so much about the importance of using science to guide policy decisions. The forum was my chance to convince people how important it was to make sure there was more than one scientist in Congress, especially with Donald Trump as president. Everything he did was a threat not only to the minimal environmental protections we had in place but to science itself.

Four male candidates surrounded me. They didn't seem to notice.

I tried to maintain my composure and refocus on what I would say to all these people. Unfortunately, the hot flashes had a habit of wrecking my concentration. If I let it distract me, I would embarrass myself in front of them. The hot flash subsided, or maybe I just forgot about it. I don't think anyone noticed. Or perhaps they just thought I was nervous.

Hot flashes are common. There it is, I said it.

As I sat down to write this chapter in another cold February, I realized I dreaded this subject. I'm still feeling queasy about sharing my experience while campaigning above. I didn't relish the thought of addressing aging, even though I know it is essential to discuss openly.

WOMEN DON'T SEEM TO WANT TO TALK ABOUT MENOPAUSE

Most women don't talk about aging or menopause in public. As I prepared for this chapter, I searched for public statements by scientists, congresswomen, businesswomen, or female academics to see what they said about menopause. I didn't find much. While eighty-eight women over the age of fifty held seats in the 117th Congress, I thought it was interesting that I couldn't find a single reference of any of them talking about personal challenges with aging or menopause.

Dr. Vivian Diller, a psychologist and author of the book *Face It*, said even in the privacy of her office, she found it hard to get women to talk about menopause and their feelings. She said anxiety, confusion, lethargy, and depression might result from hormonal changes during menopause (Diller, n.d.). Dr. Lila Nachtigall, professor of obstetrics and gynecology at NYU's Grossman School of Medicine, shared that even though she lived in the same house when her mother was experiencing menopause, they never discussed it. She said it was taboo; "You were supposed to suffer in silence" (Grose, 2021). One possible reason this taboo still exists, especially for women, is that aging presents an identity crisis. Dr. Diller said acknowledging aging might be an admission of weakness or defeat for some women (Diller, n.d.). Dr. Diller said women were reluctant to talk about aging because they felt vulnerable with the loss of an empowered self-image and control. Accepting the reality and thinking about or discussing menopausal symptoms may acknowledge that they are no longer "cool" or attractive, especially to men and younger women (Diller, n.d.). We fear becoming the frail granny image painted by a society that embraces and celebrates youthfulness.

As it was for me, the symptoms of menopause can be troubling; they typically arrive just as female scientists mature in their careers and break into leadership positions. It's estimated that about 20 to 40 percent of menopausal women experience hot flashes and night sweats just as they are entering top leadership roles in their careers (Hardy et al., 2018). "Moderating that high-profile panel, in front of two hundred industry experts, should have been a career highlight. It was a disaster," said a forty-six-year-old biotech vice president (Patterson, 2020). "Those years of confusion, self-doubt, and severe anxiety practically killed my entire career," said a fifty-one-year-old tech executive (Patterson, 2020). When Angie McKaig experienced menopausal symptoms at work, she said she "realized how few people actually talk about [it] [...] so I have tried to normalize it" (Grose, 2021).

WHAT ARE THE BENEFITS OF AGE DIVERSITY?

Organizations have focused on ethnicity and gender diversity while overlooking age diversity (HR Cloud, 2021). Normalizing aging and its challenges, like menopause, will help change the narratives that are barriers to female scientists contributing to the workforce as we age.

Women thrive financially, physically, and emotionally when work cultures prioritize age diversity. However, as discussed in the previous chapter, the opportunity cost for women can be very high in reduced wages, social security benefits, and retirement funds after they leave the work-force or reduce their hours to become caregivers for children or family members. Unlike men, who are typically less impacted by juggling work and parenting, mature female scientists have a lot of catching up to do. As a result, many can't afford to retire, an expensive prospect (Bersin and Chamorro-Premuzic, 2019). In one survey, 28 percent of those aged sixty-three to sixty-seven said they planned to delay their retirement in 2020 (Scott, 2021).

Josh Bersin and Tomas Chamorro-Premuzic asked, "Why would we want to retire if we love our work" (Bersin and Chamorro-Premuzic, 2019)? They quote Steven Hawking, who stated that "Work gives you meaning and purpose, and life is empty without it." Continuing to work "represents an opportunity to give value to others and the community." They noted working "gives you a network of friends and associates to be with; and it gives you something to do with your intellectual and physical energy" (Bersin and Chamorro-Premuzic, 2019).

With experience, female scientists gain knowledge and expertise—the main predictors of job performance—and the growth increases even beyond eighty. In addition, traits like drive and curiosity are catalysts for new skill acquisition, even during late adulthood (Bersin and Chamorro-Premuzic, 2019). Age diversity benefits organizations in several important ways (Saba and Diker, 2021; HR Cloud, 2021; Bersin and Chamorro-Premuzic, 2019):

- Mature workers offer a wide range of experience, knowledge, and resources to navigate an array of tasks and situations effectively and efficiently, creating a more stable workplace.

- Experienced workers improve productivity by teaching others to work smarter, not harder.
- Age diversity improves worker loyalty and reduces employee turnover rates. A global study focused on gender issues in the workplace concludes that if at least one woman is in a senior leadership role in an organization, other women are three times more likely to move into open senior leadership positions (Accenture, 2018).
- A company's odds of success increase with increasing numbers of female executives at the vice president and director levels (Thomas et al., 2021). According to *Women at the Wheel*, a 2012 report by Dow Jones, 61 percent of start-ups with five or more women are successful (Canning, Haque, and Wang, 2012).
- Female scientists gain experience that engenders wisdom that can be helpful for more junior scientists. Mentorship by experienced workers increased the overall skill set of the workforce and resulted in higher productivity and individual performance. Kejal Macdonald, vice president of marketing for ICON by THINX, said, "Older women have undoubtedly seen a lot of ups and downs throughout their lives. And this life experience is valuable, allowing them to notice patterns and bring perspective to the business world that is all but impossible to learn in any other way" (Accenture, 2018).
- Organizations experience more innovation, producing better outcomes, efficiency, and improved internal processes with age diversity.
- Age-diverse groups with different experiences exercise better communication than non-diverse groups, which translates into a better understanding of the target audience and increased sales.

There's room for improved gender-age diversity in US organizations. A recent analysis found that women hold only around 25 percent of C-suite positions. Only 6 percent of CEO spots are held by women, unchanged from 2018 (Stevenson and Kaplan, 2019). Jane Stevenson, global leader of Korn Ferry's CEO Succession Services, said, "In every industry we analyzed, there's a tremendous need for improvement to bring more women to the C-suite" (Patterson, 2020).

AGE CAN SIDELINE CAREER ASPIRATIONS FOR FEMALE SCIENTISTS

"As women show visible signs of aging, they are viewed as less competent and less marketable. They definitely feel isolated. They have all this expertise, but nobody values it anymore," said Bonnie Marcus, an executive coach (Place, 2021).

Some of these fears are warranted.

A study conducted by the National Institutes of Health (NIH) in 2011 found that older women are generally less successful at earning grants intended for established scientists (Rosenwald, 2011). Grant money is essential for career progression in academia. However, the study found a lack of grant funding awarded to older female scientists even though women are well-represented in early-career grant programs.

In addition, experience and expertise seem to be detrimental only to women, but not so for their male counterparts. As a result, when older female scientists try to assume higher positions, return to the workforce, or change jobs when they are older, they "are overqualified" or "they will not fit into our culture" or they "will take a lot of sick days."

I talked with Dr. Michelle Fiscus, a physician and former medical director of the Tennessee Vaccine-Preventable Diseases and Immunization Program at the Tennessee Department of Health, who rejected the notion that overqualification was a legitimate excuse for not hiring older female scientists. On the contrary, she said, "Isn't it my decision whether or not to accept the job? If I'm overqualified but willing to take the position for the pay, doesn't it benefit the organization?" She was fired because she sent a letter to the state's vaccine providers clarifying that they could administer vaccines to minors under Tennessee Law without their parent or guardian present. Recently she started her own health care consulting company.

Once older women leave the workforce "they have a terrible time getting rehired, largely because of age discrimination, which [while] against the law, is directed particularly at women who are past the age where society deems them attractive," wrote Lisa Miller (Miller, 2015).

Danielle[9] had decades of experience as a nuclear scientist, but she couldn't get an interview when she left her previous position, much less a job. So, she decided to try an experiment to test whether age was a factor causing her inability to get a job or even an interview. Danielle then removed anything from her resume that made her look older and sent it out to prospective employers. The positive response was immediate, and she soon found herself in a new position that paid her well and was commensurate with her qualifications.

Supporting Danielle's experience, a 2015 study found that fictional resumes for younger women received a much higher rate of callbacks than resumes for older women, regardless of the position advertised. The study sent fictitious resumes to forty thousand job advertisements in a dozen cities. The

---

9   A pseudonym, as she requested that I not use her real name.

authors concluded that "the evidence of discrimination against older women is strong and robust" (Neumark, Burn, and Button, 2017).

THERE IS EVIDENCE THAT AGE DISCRIMINATION IS ON THE RISE FOR FEMALE SCIENTISTS

Lynda Gratton, coauthor of *The 100 Year Life: Living and Work in an Age of Longevity*, thinks ageism is far worse for women than sexism. According to the National Science Board, the median age of scientists in the workforce increased from forty years old in 1993 to forty-three years old in 2015 (National Science Board, 2018). Gratton wrote that ageism at work begins at age forty for women, coinciding with perimenopause, and forty-five for men. She said, "At that point, the employer no longer considers the worker for promotion or training" (Barnes, 2019).

With an aging workforce demographic, age discrimination is likely a growing issue impacting female scientists. But only 59 percent of men say they have not experienced age discrimination in the workforce, while 59 percent of women reported they have. While about 90 percent of older workers suspected they had experienced age discrimination in the workplace, almost all instances went unreported (Place, 2021).

Between 2011 and 2020, cost-cutting measures inordinately impacted the National Institute of Child Health and Human Development (NICHHD)'s female scientists. According to annual reports and public announcements, the number of woman-run labs fell from 23 percent to 13 percent (43 percent reduction), while male-run labs were only cut 28 percent from 61 to 44 percent. At the time, the agency had between 3 to 20 percent fewer female scientist-run laboratories compared to other leading children's research institutions.

In 2014, nine senior female scientists at the NICHHD filed complaints against the scientific director, Constantine Stratakis, alleging gender and age discrimination. The complaints alleged that the paucity of female laboratory directors also impacted their research, which ironically gutted gynecological studies for adult women (Wadman, 2020). Deborah Dixon, a lawyer with Gomez Trial Attorneys, expressed concern about the number of complaints received against the director. She said the organization is an "environment that is not welcoming or fair toward women because, statistically speaking, there are going to be many other women who haven't come forward and haven't complained" (Wadman, 2020). Stratakis left the agency in 2020 to take another position at McGill University.

In 2017, at the prominent Salk Institute, only four of the thirty-two full professors were female (Pickett, 2019). In 2017, three senior female faculty members alleged sexual harassment and age discrimination misconduct in a case claiming that an "'old boys' club' of senior faculty restricted their access to funds, laboratory resources, and influence" (Pickett, 2019). Female scientists were given smaller offices in the basement with fewer resources and staff than men, regardless of their tenure with the Institute. They alleged that over seven years, the Institute hired 3.75 men for every woman. "I could see even then that I was not going to be in the leadership. That was not going to happen because of my gender," said Dr. Pamela Mellon.

In July of 2017, the Salk Institute issued a statement in which they attempted to smear the female scientists saying they "long remained within the bottom quartile of [their] peers and failed to publish a single paper in any of the most respected scientific publications" (Pickett, 2019). A backlash ensued after the Salk Institute case, with thirty-seven prominent researchers, including two Nobel Laureates, signing onto a public rebuke of the Institution's statement. The Nobel Prize winner Dr. Carol Greider wrote, "The next generation of scientists is watching, and many are choosing not to pursue a career in science, where they feel they will not have support" (Smith, 2019).

Dr. Holly Ingraham, professor of pharmacology at the University of California, San Francisco, who was previously a postdoctoral fellow at the Salk, said that "similar problems exist everywhere." Key figures at the Salk had "instilled a culture that consistently stacked the odds against women" (Pickett, 2019). Dr. Nancy Hopkins, a molecular biologist at MIT, said, "Hopefully, institutions will learn from this that they must deal with these situations" (Ledford, 2018). Two of the three female scientists remain at Salk, but Dr. Emerson found another position at another high-profile institution.

Attorney Patricia Barnes, a consultant on employment discrimination, said, "Women are the primary victims of age discrimination in hiring, which means that women are driven out of the workplace earlier than men and have a much more difficult time finding a way back" (Barnes, 2019). So, bringing a sexual harassment or discrimination complaint against their employer can be a death knell for their career.

Dr. Sara Mednick, a cognitive scientist at the University of California, Irvine, said, "Males have dominated science for a long time, so there's almost a cultural norm of treating women as second-class citizens. To repair that, [institutions] need an enlightened leadership to not be in denial, to acknowledge this and make real changes to support women" (Ledford, 2018).

While bringing these cases to the public consciousness was likely challenging for all involved, it is vital to highlight the need to address these issues head-on for the benefit of future generations of scientists.

YOUNGING[10] AGING AND WORKFORCE RETENTION

Flexible work schedules, job sharing, and paid family leave are investments that will pay off in the long term. When younger women see older women who have stayed the course and built their careers, they are more likely to see themselves being successful and stay with organizations.

These policy shifts are significant.

Dr. Amy Lui Abel and Dr. Diane Lim of The Conference Board said, "US businesses should put particular focus on retaining older women. Now and even more so in the future, increasing their participation would create substantial economic opportunity. To realize that opportunity, more companies should consider making flexible work arrangements a staple of their employee recruitment and engagement strategy" (Abel and Lim, 2018).

Experience can provide benefits to organizations and more junior staff that helps build the knowledge foundation necessary to address the challenges that we will collectively face in the future. We must arrest gender stereotypes and normalize age diversity so female scientists are engaged and help to innovate solutions and build resilience. To identify needed change, we must examine the complex issues and challenges encountered, mainly by female scientists during the COVID-19 pandemic.

---

10   Younging is a geologic term used while analyzing the relative age of sedimentary rocks. Here, it is a tongue-in-cheek reference to a possible new use of the word.

PART III

WHERE DO WE
GO FROM HERE?

CHAPTER 11

HITTING THE WALL

—

"Women are easier targets than men.
I think being a younger female, I'm an easy target."

—MARIA VAN KERKHOVE, WORLD HEALTH
ORGANIZATION EPIDEMIOLOGIST

On March 27, 2020, I rushed my husband to the local hospital emergency room in the neighboring town. He was having trouble breathing; I thought he had COVID-19. Unfortunately, as the hospitals were all in lockdown, I couldn't go inside with him. I sat in the car in the parking lot, waiting. A few hours later, he called me from inside with shocking news: he had leukemia. He asked me to run home and pick up a toothbrush and a few other items for him before they transported him to Boston in an ambulance. I don't remember driving home or gathering his things. I only remember saying goodbye to him as they put his stretcher into the ambulance.

As if the diagnosis of acute leukemia weren't enough, the stressed hospital staff, with the COVID-19 patients, new protocols, lack of personal protective equipment, and the constant drone of helicopters bringing critically ill patients to the roof of the hospital compounded the fear.

What if he survived his cancer only to get COVID-19 in the hospital?

At first, he was in the emergency room while they waited for the results of another COVID-19 test and treated him for his acute condition. Then, at some point, he ended up on the oncology floor. It was all a blur. The nurses were very stressed but recognized how challenging the COVID-19 restrictions were on all of us. The nurses propped my husband's cell phone on his tray near him, and I watched him from FaceTime on my cell phone. Sometimes, I thought the nurses appreciated that I was watching over him, even if by cell phone. At all times, I kept two cell phones with me; at night, I propped a cell phone near my pillow, another ready to make calls to family, nurses, and doctors.

The night after he was admitted, while he was on the oncology floor, I watched as his whole body heaved to take in a breath that I feared would be his last. The nurses and doctors were stressed and perhaps distracted, especially on the night shift. His breathing got so bad that, on the advice of my brother-in-law, I paged the top doctor on call; they moved him to the intensive care unit (ICU) and put him on a ventilator. Later, the doctors told me if he had been admitted just a few days later, no ventilators would have been available due to the influx of COVID-19 patients.

They took my husband off the ventilator a day later, and he returned to the oncology floor. His condition was so acute, they immediately initiated chemotherapy treatments. For the next five weeks, I could not visit the hospital. I couldn't be there to help with even the most minor things, like adjusting his pillow or making sure he had ice water while he was undergoing intense chemotherapy treatment. Since all I could do for him was bring a few items from home, the nurses graciously met me for a few moments in the parking lot to receive them. They often had tears in their eyes when they saw mine. They were sad they couldn't hug me and said all the precautions, and lack of contact with families, were difficult for them too. The first time I saw his doctor's face without a mask was during a virtual conference well after the intense hospitalizations were complete.

The refusal of some to be vaccinated or their complaints about wearing masks or other layered strategies to prevent people from getting COVID-19 still infuriates me. What if the hospital had no ventilator for my husband when he needed it because the last available one was being used on a willfully ignorant person who caught COVID-19 but who was as much a victim of the disease of cynical political manipulation as of the physical pandemic? It was, and is, incredibly frustrating to see people reject science-based approaches to control the pandemic, especially since COVID-19 is perilous for people with vulnerabilities like cancer.

While the experience was traumatizing, I realized many more have not seen their family members come home from the hospital during this pandemic. Unfortunately, my personal story is not unlike many others who faced health care and emotional challenges during the pandemic.

FEMALE SCIENTISTS SPEAK OUT

The pandemic caused stress and lost jobs, making existing structural inequalities more apparent. Many female scientists spoke out against President Trump's lack of preparedness, inequities, and the anti-science narrative of his minions in the press and on social media platforms.

At the beginning of the pandemic, health care workers and physicians I knew from my legislative and campaign experiences reached out to me to express their concerns about the national and my state's response to the pandemic. As a result, we formed a task force that was outspoken about the need for data transparency and appropriate government agency response. The task force became a nonprofit organization. NH Science and Public Health focused on developing science in response to community concerns. An outgrowth is a podcast called *Ms Information* with a mission of combating pseudoscience by communicating and celebrating science and correcting Trumpian and other politically motivated misinformation.

Many other women spoke out too.

Dr. Michelle Fiscus had built a medical practice with her partner in a Tennessee county with one of the lowest immunization rates in the state. She told me she was shocked when suddenly parents of longtime patients began to question the need for vaccines. Dr. Fiscus told me, "I would always ask myself how these parents could think that I would recommend to purposely inject something into their kids that was bad for them. Sometimes, we have had this relationship for eleven or even sixteen years, and they're actually questioning my intentions now? Suddenly I had an existential crisis. I helped you raise your child for eleven years, but you think that I'm a monster that would suggest that you give them something that I know is harmful to them." After seventeen years, Dr. Fiscus decided to close her practice and move on.

In January 2019, she became the medical director of Tennessee's immunization program. Dr. Fiscus told me she was excited to improve the state's vaccination program. While director, she dealt with three major outbreaks in two and a half years. When the pandemic started, it wasn't uncommon for her to work ninety hours per week rolling out the state's vaccination program. Dr. Fiscus said, "The work was exhausting but not demoralizing." But in 2020, the political culture in Tennessee made Dr. Fiscus's work both exhausting and demoralizing.

Dr. Fiscus conducted social media campaigns to overcome the hesitancy issues previously observed in her practice. But when she wrote a memo notifying physicians about the provision in Tennessee law that allows doctors to administer vaccines to fourteen- to seventeen-year-olds without parental consent, she encountered trouble. She said she wanted to make sure that physicians would understand the law and not hesitate to vaccinate this age group that saw a very high number of COVID-19 cases. However, Dr. Fiscus faced criticism, roadblocks, and difficulty with her female supervisor, whom she thought would support her efforts. She also said her male mentor "told me he was 'fighting for me,' but at the end of the day, it was his name at the bottom of the bogus justification letter released to the media about my firing. It turns out my mentor did not have the convictions I had credited him with," she said. In September 2021, Dr. Fiscus filed a defamation lawsuit against the state health department for statements her bosses made about her, causing her to move to a different state for employment (Jackson, 2021). In January 2022, a judge ruled against Dr. Fiscus (Wenzel, 2022).

AN UGLY TURN

During the pandemic, social media attacks on female scientists who spoke out about appropriate steps to protect public health took an ugly turn; the threats were laced with misogyny and promises of sexual violence. Female scientists were accused of being murderers and received rape and death threats and threats against their families. They were ferociously attacked on social media and by e-mail for speaking about necessary precautions (Bendix, 2022). Among scientists who responded to a survey conducted by *Nature*, 63 percent said they used Twitter to comment on aspects of COVID-19, and around one-third of those stated they were "always" or "usually" attacked on the platform. Six scientists said they were physically attacked (Nogrady, 2021).

Dr. Saskia V. Popescu, an infection-prevention epidemiologist with George Mason University, explained, "The amount of harassment we get on social media [...] is horrible. It's rare if I go a week without a sexual assault threat and even more rare if I go three days without a random creep showing up in my direct messages" (Gold, 2020). She noted that after she said we shouldn't call it the "China Virus," she received forty thousand comments and rape and death threats for weeks. Infectious-diseases physician Dr. Krutika Kuppalli, from the Medical University of South Carolina in Charleston, had been in her new job for barely a week in September 2020 when someone called her home and threatened to kill her.

After a second death threat, the police officer who visited Dr. Kuppalli suggested she should get herself a gun (Nogrady, 2021). Dr. Maia Majumder, a professor at Boston Children's Hospital and Harvard Medical School, draws a contrast with her white colleagues, noting that she received e-mails full of anti-science rhetoric as well as racist and Islamophobic slurs (Gold, 2020). Dr. Angela Rasmussen, virologist and an affiliate of the Georgetown Center for Global Health Science and Security, said social media attacks could take a toll on female scientists. "It does not relieve my anxiety or improve my state of mind to receive rape or death threats, or just to hear that I'm ugly, fat, old, stupid, or whatever else random people on the Internet like to say to insult women," she said (Gold, 2020).

Some female scientists receive troubling threats by US Mail. For example, Dr. Natalie Dean, assistant professor of biostatistics at the University of Florida, called the University police when she received a shocking package that contained Ziploc bags full of tissues of sweat and saliva labeled with different body parts (Nogrady, 2021).

Sometimes the attacks on female scientists discount their expertise; sometimes, the feedback comes from experts in the field, often men, who have even gone as far as e-mailing their bosses to demand tweets be removed. Dr. Popescu said, "The men quoted all the time are often wrong and sensationalist, and when we work to correct it, we're called 'shrill' or 'petty' versus when a man critiques a non-expert, he's applauded. That's been mind-blowing" (Gold, 2020). Dr. Rasmussen said, "Apparently, my PhD in microbiology and fifteen years of experience studying emerging viruses is insufficient for many random men on Twitter to resist the urge to explain my field of study to me and get offended when I call that out" (Gold, 2020).

But some say, to some extent, this harassment of female scientists reflects their rising status as public figures. "The more prominent you are, the more abuse you're going to get," said historian Dr. Heidi Tworek at the University of British Columbia in Vancouver, Canada, who is studying online abuse of health communicators in the pandemic (Nogrady, 2021).

The constant criticism and attacks took an emotional toll on many women scientists. For example, Dr. Rasmussen said, "I've experienced insomnia, chronic sleep deprivation, fitful sleep when I get it, massive anxiety, severe stress, and depression. This is not only because of the sense of existential dread that the pandemic has caused but also frustration at being able to see the negative outcomes of our country's inadequate responses before they happen and being forced to watch them happen anyway" (Gold, 2020).

When Donald Trump left office, many public health scientists breathed a sigh of relief. Early on, the Biden administration signaled a priority to restore science-based decision-making. President Biden wrote his top science advisor an open letter urging him to "refresh and reinvigorate our national science and technology strategy to set us on a strong course for the next seventy-five years" (Thompson, 2022a). He also issued a warning on his first day in office: "Anyone who disrespected their colleagues would be fired 'On the spot. No ifs, ands, or buts'" (Thompson, 2022). But, when multiple women complained about bullying, a two-month investigation found credible evidence that the top science advisor, Eric Lander, bullied and demeaned female employees (Thompson, 2022). At first, Lander apologized for his behavior, and the administration stood by him. Later that same day, when *Politico* broke a story about the investigation findings, Lander resigned (Thompson, 2022b). Lander should have been fired immediately to signal a sincere pledge for zero tolerance.

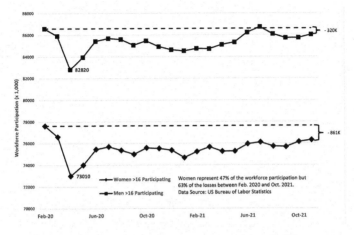

MEN V. WOMEN, COVID-19 PANDEMIC JOB LOSSES
THROUGH NOVEMBER 2021.

WOMEN HIT THE COVID-19 WALL HARDER THAN MEN

The pandemic's disproportionate impact on women was measurable. The pandemic disrupted the lives of women more than men. Under normal circumstances, women had to wear many hats. When schools closed, workplaces went remote, health care and caregiver networks were disrupted, and family members became ill, women faced tremendous additional challenges. Women have difficulty balancing increasing workloads and increased family responsibility and either leave the workforce or consider leaving the workforce in great numbers (Deloitte, 2021; Ammerman and Groysberg, 2020). Between March and September of 2020, an estimated 4.5 million people left the workforce, 61 percent of whom were women. In September 2020 alone, an estimated 865,000 women had left the workforce, representing approximately 82 percent of the losses in the US (Gogoi, 2020). Almost a year and a half later, the workforce losses for women still exceeded those for men. While there has been some recovery, as of January 2022, there were still 1.1 million fewer women who returned to work (Smith, 2022). Even though 467,000 jobs were added in January 2022, only 39,000 of those were filled by women (Smith, 2022). As a result, more women than men have left their jobs, and many still have not returned because of the continual flow of variants and subsequent waves of COVID-19 infections.

In addition, women of color and lesbian, gay, bisexual, transexual, queer or questioning, intersectional, and asexual (LGBTQIA+) were more likely to have suffered negative impacts due to the pandemic (Movement Advancement Project, 2020). Pre-pandemic, STEM retention for sexually diverse undergraduate students was 7 percent lower than heterosexuals (Hughes, 2018). When the pandemic hit, about one-third of the 3.4 million LGBTQ students reported financial support and housing disruptions that affected their ability to remain students. In addition, about one in five reported taking a leave of absence due to the pandemic (Conron, O'Neill, and Sears, 2021).

THE PANDEMIC EXACERBATED THE MOTHERHOOD PENALTY FOR STEM WOMEN.

Gender disparities caused by responsibility imbalances put women at a disadvantage when compared to men, a factor that could eventuate professional career setbacks. For example, a survey of 224 STEM women by Mothers in Science found that over 60 percent of them said they spent more time than their spouses on homeschooling or caregiving during the pandemic (Mothers in Science, 2019). In addition, the COVID-19-lockdown–related effect impacted female scientists' capacity to publish. Another study found a 20 percent increase in male-scientist-led grant proposals but decreased female scientists' submissions during the pandemic's early part (Wu, 2021). One study concluded that the

"COVID-19-lockdown-related effect on women's capacity to publish [...] could damage careers going forward" (Ribarovska et al., 2021; Staniscuaski et al., 2021).

Moreover, the pandemic's impact had a measurable effect on women with children. One study found a direct relationship between the number and age of young dependents and a proportional negative impact on publishing for female scientists. Female scientists with at least one younger child could devote 17 percent less time to research and 3 percent less time spent on research when they had more than one child (Myers et al., 2020).

"It's become clear that organizations need to address these roles and help find a way for women scientists to still have room to succeed at work," said Dr. Edith Heard, European Molecular Biology Laboratory (EMBL) director general (Kupec, 2020).

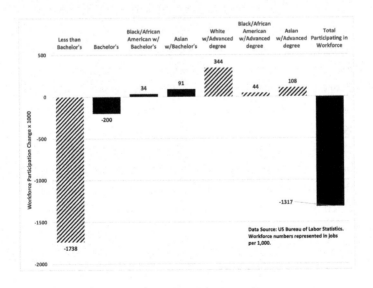

EDUCATIONAL ATTAINMENT MITIGATED RECOVERY
FROM THE PANDEMIC LOSSES FOR WOMEN.

Workforce participation losses between February 2020 and September 2021 for women (69 percent) exceeded losses by men (31 percent); however, educational attainment partially mitigated those losses for women (U.S. Bureau of Labor Statistics, 2022). While available US Labor Department data do not differentiate the occupations of degreed women, it is likely a good indicator of STEM women in the workforce since, as of 2019, about 47 percent of women with college degrees work in STEM fields (National Science Foundation, 2021).

Between February 2020 and September 2021, the job losses for women were directly proportional to educational attainment; women with less than a bachelor's degree lost the highest proportion of jobs, while women with bachelor's degrees still experienced job losses but women with advanced degrees added jobs. Black women with bachelor's degrees recovered fifty thousand jobs compared to February 2020.

White women with advanced degrees recovered the most jobs as of September 2021, followed by Asian women. Between February 2020 and September 2021, women with advanced degrees, regardless of race, contributed to an overall *gain* of 496,000 jobs, while women with less than a bachelor's degree *lost* 1,738,000 jobs and seventy-five thousand women with a bachelor's degree were still out of work. These data support the need to provide conditions that encourage women to reach their higher education goals to remain resilient during challenging periods.

THERE'S A BETTER WAY

The pandemic uncovered and laid bare inequalities that disproportionally impacted women and female scientists. But the data show that if employers create a culture that supports and enables women to succeed, they will have a more productive and motivated workforce and likely retain female scientists. "Women are going to continue to bear the brunt of pandemic job losses. I would hope that almost two years into this crisis, we would be closer to where we were pre-pandemic—we want women to recoup their losses just like men have at this point, but that's not happening, and that's a real crisis," said Jasmine Tucker of the National Women's Law Center (Smith, 2022). A year later, not much has improved.

As organizations look to rebuild their workplaces, those prioritizing diversity, equity, and inclusion in their policies and culture and providing tangible support for the women in their workforces will be more resilient against future disruptions. As of August 2021, 55 percent of women and men in the workforce said they want to seek new employment over the coming year (Foster 2021). "Pandemic-inspired changes, including the ability to work remotely and/or from home, have transformed mindsets and expectations for many workers," said Mark Hamrick, Bankrate senior economic analyst and Washington bureau chief (Foster, 2021).

Ms. Shanika Amarakoon, an engineer and mother of a young girl, said that while it has undoubtedly been a challenge to juggle childcare and work responsibilities, operating remotely during the pandemic has made people "much more accepting and understanding. I feel like it's humanized everyone." In addition, people are getting used to seeing a glimpse into one's personal life, with children, dogs, and cats making appearances on Zoom calls. "It seems that people are just more human; I feel like [employers and colleagues] have more understanding and compassion for all the things that we're trying to juggle," said Ms. Amarakoon.

FLEXIBILITY IS KEY

It's time to reflect on the changes that would improve and encourage all women, not only those privileged, to enter and stay in careers. If workers feel they can address personal challenges with employers without fear of retribution, pandemic recovery will quicken. In 2021, nearly one in five women said they never want to return to work in person (Cassella, 2021). According to a study by Deloitte, fewer than half of women are satisfied with their current jobs, and 51 percent are less optimistic about their career prospects than before the pandemic. "Our survey respondents are clear about what needs to be done to reverse the pandemic's disproportionate effects on working women" (Parmelee and Codd, 2021).

Offering employees higher wages, more paid time off, flexible hours, and more remote work could help keep women in the workforce or help them return to work, allowing them to manage caregiving responsibilities better. Employers who have adapted to the challenges posed by the pandemic were able to retain workers, and those workers reported overall that they were happier with their employment situation.

Dr. Birnbaum told me she helped establish a program to create flexible work environments for female postdoctoral students who have babies. The program allows female scientists to work part-time for two years after giving birth. But, Dr. Birnbaum said, "In the end, a few years of part-time work while having kids isn't consequential to your career in the long run, so women shouldn't worry about the impact of part-time work [for a few years] on their career trajectory."

Dr. Alisa Stephens, a biostatistician at the University of Pennsylvania, thinks universities should help scientists by adding an extra year to the time allotted to earn tenure (Mandavilli, 2021). Some institutions and the US Government have made accommodations for female scientists, including tenure extensions, but some caution that gender-neutral policies exacerbate preexisting inequalities (Antecol, Bedard, and Stearns, 2018).

Programs that provide economic support for women to enter and stay in STEM academic programs are essential. Unless women have the financial means, the stressors and rigors of higher education and research can be too much. Often women leave academia when faced with a decision to provide for themselves and their families.

Unfortunately, a global pandemic hit when the US had the most anti-science president of all time. Governments were caught flat-footed in the early days of the pandemic with inadequate personal protective equipment and knowledge of virus transmission and emergency response procedures and plans. Politics and science denial made social media a war zone for many scientists, and innocent victims suffered collateral damage, as they do in all wars. I can testify from my own experiences that anti-science ignorance and irrationalism caused extra stress when my husband faced severe health challenges in the middle of the pandemic.

Perhaps the silver lining of the pandemic will be that it offered a rebalancing of life and work challenges for female scientists. Neneng Goenadi, Accenture Indonesia Country managing director, said, "In companies with cultures that include the workplace factors that help women advance, men thrive too, and we all rise together" (Accenture, 2018).

CHAPTER 12

CALLING ALL HUMANITY

—

"Humanity is called to recognize the need for change of lifestyle, production, and consumption, in order to combat this warming or at least the human causes which produce or aggravate it."

—POPE FRANCIS

Sometimes you don't accomplish what you set out to do—but there is a silver lining.

A confluence of academic, legislative, and advocacy work built on my professional experience helped me connect important issues. As my friend Caroline said to me many times, "You know how to connect the dots; most people don't know how to do that. So, you have to draw it out for them."

Between 2017 and the election in 2018, as a candidate for an open congressional seat, I crisscrossed New Hampshire talking about how climate change is a "threat multiplier."

Climate change multiplies challenges we already face like poverty, hunger, disease, and lack of access to clean water. As people become desperate and structural inequalities deepen, violence and political crises lead to migration as they try to escape.

As the sea level rises, the saltwater intrudes into the freshwater aquifer, limiting drinkable water availability. As the sea level rises, the saltwater washes over the land surface or roads and intrudes into groundwater, also polluting the freshwater aquifer. In addition, since saltwater is heavier than groundwater, landfills engineered for deeper water tables and other shallow contamination like gasoline spills can contaminate water sources with groundwater rise. The effects of climate change are already impacting all seacoast areas, threatening the quantity and quality of drinking water, a problem that will worsen as climate change progresses.

Along the New Hampshire and Massachusetts coastlines, the sea level is seven inches higher than it was in 1950, and the rate of increase in sea-level rise has sped up to approximately one inch every ten years (Sea Level Rise.org, n.d.). As a result, there is more and more flooding every winter that coincides with more severe winter storms. Sea level rise threatens water supplies in all coastal areas.

In 2019, I was selected to be a state co-chair for a presidential candidate in New Hampshire and to be a delegate by the candidate to the national convention. Since climate change is a critical existential threat, every chance I got, I talked about climate change when I introduced the candidate. I was also able to make cancer prevention, drinking water protection, and climate change the focus of campaign forums and panels.

A WOMAN DISCOVERED CLIMATE CHANGE
(I BET YOU DIDN'T KNOW THAT)

As in other areas of science, a male scientist took credit for Eunice Newton Foote's foundational climate science work. In 1856, Ms. Foote, an American scientist, inventor, and women's rights campaigner, was the first to identify the effect of solar radiation on gases. Her paper entitled "Circumstances affecting the heat of the Sun's rays" is the first paper on climate change (Foote, 1856). John Tyndall, whose work appeared three years after Foote's foundational work, has traditionally been recognized as one of the founders of climate science. Ms. Foote's discovery was never referenced in Tyndall's work (Jackson, 2019).

Besides the measurable sea-level rise, the temperature of the earth's atmosphere is also rising. It's now about 1.1°C warmer than in the late 1800s, with the last decade (2011 to 2020) having been the warmest on record (United Nations, n.d.).

Scientists know that human activity influences the trajectory of climate change, and science-based decision-making can mitigate the severity of impacts. Scientists say we are at a fork in the road and face two divergent pathways (shown as broken arrows in the figure by Steffen et al., 2018). The further we proceed down the path to the "Hothouse Earth," driven by human emissions of greenhouse gases, the harder it will be, if not impossible, to reverse climate change (Steffen et al., 2018).

Dr. Katharine Hayhoe, an atmospheric science professor at Texas Tech University, said, "The data tell us the planet is warming; the science is clear that humans are responsible; the impacts we're seeing today are already serious" (Hayhoe, n.d.).

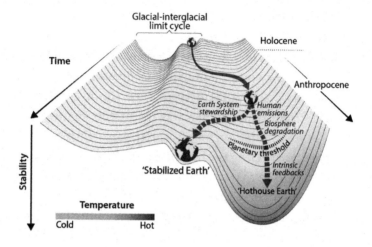

FORK IN THE ROAD, HOTHOUSE EARTH OR STABILIZED EARTH?
FROM (STEFFEN ET AL., 2018).

"THERE'S NO TIME TO WAIT"

Priya Shukla, a PhD student at the University of California, Davis, is studying the impact of climate change on marine oysters. She is a passionate young scientist of color, and in chapter 4 I discussed how she often felt unrecognized and unempowered in her work.

Ms. Shukla said the impacts of climate change on oysters were already visible. In a podcast interview, Ms. Shukla said she felt tightness in her chest and it was hard to breathe after reading a new scientific paper on oyster deaths from unusually warm water (Gladstone, 2019). Ms. Shukla told me that the paper documented that 90 to 100 percent of tiny oysters had died every summer. She saw it like a fire alarm that no one else seemed to hear, that climate change was already causing devastating effects on oyster populations. The millimeter-sized oysters can't eat until they create their shells, which must happen during the first twelve to twenty-four hours of life, or they die. Ms. Shukla told me the warming water makes the baby oysters especially vulnerable to a virus that impedes their ability to form shells.

Consequently, she told me she feels a sense of urgency to share her results with oyster fishermen now rather than later. Sharing work ahead of journal publication is highly unusual for scientific work. But Ms. Shukla told me she used her data to help oyster farmers develop strategies to overcome the viral infections. With climate change reaching a global tipping point, Ms. Shukla said she couldn't delay sharing the data until a journal publishes her work, a process that could take several years. Ms. Shukla told me, "There is a chance that I won't be done publishing until 2030." If she waited until 2030 to share her data, she feared it would be too late. The farmers needed to develop mitigation strategies now.

THE PUBLIC HEALTH AND ENVIRONMENTAL IMPACTS FROM CLIMATE CHANGE ARE ALREADY MEASURABLE

Scientists predict climate change will cause higher cancer rates, especially lung, skin, and gastrointestinal cancers (Hiatt and Beyeler, 2020). While at first, a family member with cancer may not seem like a climate change or gender issue, it most certainly is. Women are 51 percent of the population and are the primary caregivers for their children and families. When we take our kids to the doctor or state agencies, our concerns are frequently ignored or minimized, and our legitimate fears are often dismissed as unwarranted. When a family member is sickened with cancer like my husband's, or other preventable chronic diseases, the women carry the bulk of the stress and responsibility.

In addition, forest fires and other airborne pollutants and particulates associated with increased carbon dioxide levels in the atmosphere are causing increased asthma and other respiratory illnesses (Shabir, 2022). For example, after Hurricane Harvey hit the Houston area in 2017, airborne emissions from forty-six facilities exceeded state regulatory limits.

At least fourteen toxic waste sites were flooded or damaged, and almost one hundred spills of hazardous substances were reported (Griggs et al., 2017). As we experience increasingly severe and more frequent storms due to climate change, these weather events spread chemicals, gasoline, oil, and other contamination into the ground and the groundwater and drinking water. So, the threats to our drinking water are inextricably linked to climate change.

Warming climates are already expanding vector-borne disease seasons (Collaborative on Health and the Environment, 2019). For example, in April 2018, Dr. Barbara Ferrer reported that vector-borne disease seasons transmitted by mosquitos had extended at least 2.5 months, resulting in increased disease and deaths from West Nile Virus in Los Angeles County (Boston University, 2018).

The impacts of temperature extremes associated with climate change are becoming more frequent and more severe. According to recent studies, more than five million people die each year due to excessively hot or cold conditions, and heat-related deaths are rising (Lu and Cox, 2021). About 9.4 percent of global deaths each year are attributable to heat or cold exposure. The elderly, children, and people with chronic diseases have a higher-than-average risk of heat-related death (USGCRP, 2016). Because children's bodies cannot mitigate the heat as well as adults', they are less able to adapt to heat than adult bodies. As a result, cardiovascular and respiratory illnesses will worsen due to climate change, creating a vicious downward spiral of vulnerability to the effects of climate change. The impacts of climate change will affect the health of children born today throughout their lifetimes (Helldén et al., 2021; Watts et al., 2019).

WHAT CAN WE DO TO BREAK THIS VICIOUS CYCLE?

"The number one thing we can do is the exact thing that we're not doing: talk about it," said atmospheric scientist Dr. Katharine Hayhoe (TED, 2018). People have been talking about the climate crisis, but they are primarily men. For example, although gender parity improved the May to June 2021 United Nations Climate Change Conference (COP26) Subsidiary Body meetings, 60 percent of plenary speakers were male. Men spoke 74 percent of the time (U.N. Climate Change News, 2021).

Women continue to be underrepresented or excluded from necessary research, highlighting ongoing ethical and justice concerns. But the conversation about diversity and inclusivity for women and people of color is not about how vulnerable they are; it's about empowering women, hearing minorities' voices, and reversing the patriarchal and white-centered history. Viewing women as weak perpetuates the gender stereotypes and structures subjugating women to men. The inordinate impact of climate change on women is not due to inherent vulnerability "but the result of gender inequalities in the political, social, and economic realms that intersect with other axes of social disadvantages, such as race, sexuality, gender identity, and disability status" (Jeffs, 2022).

Including more female climate scientists in developing mitigation strategies could provide a complete understanding of the far-reaching implications of climate change and help determine more effective solutions. The Scottish Government and the U.N. Women at COP26 published a joint statement that called for gender parity for girls and women in climate science who have created and led innovative climate solutions at all levels (Scottish Government and U.N. Women at COP26, 2021). Female scientists made up only 8 percent of the authors of the first Intergovernmental Panel on Climate Change (IPCC) in 1990.

In 2022, women were 56 percent of the core writing team and editors for the AR6 Synthesis Report (Intergovernmental Panel on Climate Change, 2022). In addition, the 2021 *Reuters* "Hot List of 1,000 top climate scientists" only had 122 women (Tamman, 2021b). The scientists were judged by how many publications they wrote on climate change and how often other scientists, or the media, cited those papers. In chapter 5, I discussed that all metrics disproportionately favor male over female scientists.

Including female scientists in climate change work only to not give voice to women, children, and other vulnerable people disguises inequity and relegates women to a subservient position in problem-solving. Instead, female scientists should have equitable access afforded to male scientists. Dr. Maureen Raymo, a paleoclimatologist and cofounding dean of the Columbia Climate School and director of the Lamont-Doherty Earth Observatory, said, "Fostering healthy group dynamics is everyone's responsibility—we all need to do the work of making sure diverse perspectives come together in collaborative and productive ways" (Cho, 2022).

PRECAUTION LEADS TO PREVENTION AND RESILIENCY
When the pandemic hit in March of 2020, my family and many others had to maneuver through a health care system that was taxed and overloaded to obtain health care for non-COVID-related issues. The pandemic shined a light on

the importance of disease prevention and many underlying structural problems and systemic inequities.

Over the seven years before the pandemic, annual spending on cancer care tripled to more than $156B (Park and Look, 2019; Fang and Frosch, 2021), but much of that cost, as well as the untold suffering of individuals and families, could be reduced by preventing cancers in the first place. It's estimated that at least two-thirds of all cancer cases could be prevented by minimizing environmental causes (U.S. Department of Health and Human Services, 2003). Reducing cancer rates would also reduce the exposure of more vulnerable people to the effects of stressors like climate change and COVID-19 (Grandjean et al., 2020).

"When an activity raises threats of harm to human health or the environment, precautionary measures should be taken even if some cause-and-effect relationships are not fully established scientifically."

—WINGSPREAD STATEMENT (CHE, 2019)

Evaluating chemicals before the public is exposed is essential in cancer prevention. "Most people assume that chemicals have been thoroughly vetted before they enter the market. But that is not the case. And that has never been the case in the US," said Britt Erickson, a senior reporter for *Chemical and Engineering News* (Erickson, 2020). Over the last forty-seven years, the EPA has approved 54,592 new chemicals while taking steps to prevent exposure by regulating only sixty-eight chemicals under the Safe Drinking Water Act (SDWA) since 1974 (U.S. Environmental Protection Agency,

2022; Congressional Research Service, 2022). Between 2016 and 2022, the EPA rejected only twelve of 1,736 chemicals because of the potential risk to public health and safety (U.S. Environmental Protection Agency, 2022). Is the EPA protecting the public or the interests of the chemical industry?

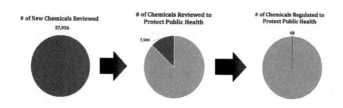

EPA CHEMICAL APPROVAL AND REGULATION PROGRESS SINCE 1974.

Dr. Kyla Bennett told me, "EPA cares more about the industry and getting their products out than it does about protecting human health and the environment."

POLICY CHANGE IS NEEDED

One female climate scientist from Quebec, Dr. Corinne Le Quéré, made it on *Reuters* "Hot List of the 1,000 top climate scientists" for her work identifying precipitous drops in carbon dioxide levels at the beginning of the COVID-19 pandemic (Tamman, 2021a). However, she expressed frustration with inaction, "For three or four years, I have worked with policymakers, and I just don't know how to make them realize they must act" (Tamman, 2021). And Pope Francis said, "There is an urgent need to develop policies that, in the next few years, the emission of carbon dioxide and other highly polluting gases can be drastically reduced, for example, substituting for fossil fuels and developing sources of renewable energy" (Francis and Oreskes, 2015).

In January of 2021, President Biden issued an executive order that outlined broad plans for addressing climate change during his administration. Unfortunately, the order doesn't go far enough. It does not call for a pause in drilling for fossil fuel on public lands rather than a long-term solution. With the recent events in Ukraine, the high cost of oil may increase the potential for oil drilling on public lands. The Executive Order does ensure that federal funds will not be used to subsidize fossil fuels directly and calls for "elimination of subsidies in the Fiscal Year 2022 budget request and thereafter" (The White House, 2021).

In October 2021, the Department of Health and Human Services (DHHS) released its Climate Adaptation and Resilience Plan (U.S. Department of Health and Human Services, 2021). The plan details interagency coordination to address data needs, climate adaptation research, and grant opportunities. It also builds "resilience to climate change-related health, economic, and other threats [...] essential to fulfilling the DHHS mission to enhance the health and well-being of all Americans." However, missing from the plan are actionable steps to improve gender diversity to ensure that women have a voice in developing comprehensive solutions and timetables that match the severity of the crisis. Like EPA's PFAS Action Plan, the DHHS plan to address the climate crisis is a good step forward; however, much more aggressive action is needed.

IT'S TIME FOR A CHANGE

While there has undoubtedly been a change for the better at the national level concerning global warming and science in general, we must press for swift and bold action to stay out of the hothouse trench. We must make sure that while some say, "Nothing will fundamentally change," an informed citizenry is critical to pushing forward for our children's future and that of future generations. There are many opportunities to track issues relating to science and climate change. But change won't happen without women. Scientists like Dr. Le Quéré and advocates have been calling for action for decades; the advocacy energy from younger generations is inspiring, and it is especially important that women's voices are raised because history suggests women, more than men, will shoulder a disproportionate share of the burdens from climate change. However, continued advocacy is necessary to bring about the change needed to reduce carbon dioxide levels in the atmosphere. Unfortunately, there has not been enough action to address this issue.

Ultimately, the time is now. It's time to arrest the dynamics that undermine female scientists. Female scientists and leaders in advocacy, politics, and the workforce need support and empowerment to push for the changes necessary to address the complex issues.

CHAPTER 13

WE CAN DO THIS!

—

*"Trusting so-called authority is not enough.
A sense of personal responsibility is what we
desperately need."*

—RACHEL CARSON

Arsenic is a colorless, odorless, and tasteless semimetal or metalloid. It was used extensively during the Victorian Age in products like wallpaper because of the beautiful colors it produced. From the Roman Empire through the Middle Ages and the Renaissance, arsenic was also used to poison political enemies and foes (Smith, n.d.). For example, before he died in 1791, Wolfgang Amadeus Mozart said he was poisoned with "Acqua Tofana" by a rival (Dash, 2015). Acqua Tofano references Giulia Tofana, who sold arsenic-laced poison to women who wished to end unhappy, forced marriages. According to historical accounts, in the mid-1600s, six hundred husbands succumbed to her poison (Whorton, 2010).

THEY KNEW BUT FAILED TO ACT

Arsenic is naturally occurring in New England bedrock and often gets into drinking water wells that tap into the hard rock groundwater (Ayotte et al., 2017). Even though arsenic in drinking water is naturally occurring due to the prevalent rock types, the high rate of bladder cancer requires action. In 2017, New Hampshire had the highest rate of bladder cancer in the nation (DHHS News, 2018), so I introduced a bill when I was a state legislator that would tighten drinking water protections for arsenic (Messmer et al., 2017). The bill was a bipartisan effort supported by Rep. Jim McConnell—R, Rep. Renny Cushing—D, Rep. Chuck Grassie—D, and a few other legislators. House Bill HB1592 compelled the environmental services department to cut the allowable limit of arsenic in drinking water by half. For comparison, while New Hampshire was idle, New Jersey had already instituted this in 2006, leading to a bladder cancer rate ten times lower than New Hampshire's in 2017.

I introduced the bill to the House Executive Departments and Administration Committee; it had already passed the House Resources, Recreation, and Development Committee. I answered questions from the committee and sat down to watch the rest of the hearing play out. But unlike all my other bills, I was surprised that the state environmental agency representative did not oppose this one. They had fought everything else I tried: my attempts to pass stricter protections on "forever chemicals" and pesticides and bottled water restrictions. It had always been my experience that the agency would start their testimony saying they have no position but then trash it.

A committee member, House Representative Jackie Cilley, asked the state environmental agency representative if they knew about the comparison I had drawn in my testimony between bladder cancer rates in New Hampshire and New Jersey and the differences between the two states for allowable arsenic exposure from drinking water. Rep. Cilley asked if he knew that New Jersey's drinking water standard passed twelve years earlier was twice as protective as ours, and, consequently, their bladder cancer rate was an order of magnitude lower than New Hampshire's. He answered yes. Then she asked him why the state agency hadn't acted if they knew about arsenic causing high rates of bladder cancer?

I was stunned to hear the regulator's response.

The regulators knew all along that the allowable levels of arsenic in drinking water protection were too lax and was causing an extraordinary rate of bladder cancer in New Hampshire. He said they did not act because there had never been a *scientific legislator* that made them do it.

I could have fallen off my chair.

Acting to protect public health is what we task our regulatory agencies to do. And we assume they are doing it, right? Because we could not get bipartisan support to directly revise the allowable level of arsenic after all of that, an amended bill passed into law that compelled the state to closely look at the appropriate level of arsenic in drinking water; in 2019, the stricter arsenic standard that I vied for finally became law. Sometimes it takes more than one shot for a good measure to pass. Hopefully, in the future, the bladder cancer rate will be one-tenth of what it is now—tied with New Jersey.

IT'S TIME TO ACT

The last two years have been a time of tremendous grief and loss; the pandemic has taken the lives of nearly one million people in the United States. Many needlessly died due to COVID-19 and ignorance of layered strategies and science-based policy to prevent disease transmission. Throughout the tragedy, steps to implement science-based mitigation strategies were weaponized and caused division along political lines. Female scientists shouldered a disproportionate burden of the attacks; they faced threats laced with misogyny and promises of sexual violence just for speaking about appropriate public health mitigation measures.

It's time to take a step back and reconsider our actions and how to protect humanity from the challenges of the future.

In 1988, Lilian Wylie, a resident of North Hampton, New Hampshire, stated she was naive to think that if something went wrong, the state would protect her, her family, and her neighbors—the meager steps taken were ineffective. The exiguous band-aids left my community and my state with high cancer rates in children and adults, twenty Superfund sites, including the toxic soup at the edge of my town.

We all want to believe there is someone else out there who knows more than we do about something, that's protecting us so we can make sure the kids get to soccer or school, so we can go to school or work and live our lives without the worry. But as Ms. Wylie recognized, the onus is on us to step forward and advocate for change.

As we face challenges that will shape the world for generations to come, we must include diverse voices to produce innovative, effective solutions that address everyone's needs, including historically and especially overlooked populations. Empowering female scientists to use their expertise with respect for their work and input is necessary to move forward.

Equitable representation includes women at the table making decisions, with diverse perspectives from their life experiences that differ from men. While progress has been made, gender parity is still an issue in government decision-making at all levels; women make up less than one-third of global governmental leadership positions (University of Pittsburgh and United Nations Development Programme, 2021).

Here are some ideas for action:

- Create an office of diversity to put more robust policies and laws in place that enforce gender quotas in governmental organizations with intrepid targets for gender parity. Models include programs implemented by Dr. Kirsty Duncan in Canada and the Athena SWAN program in the UK.
- Create incentives and support for studies that assess factors impacting LGBTQIA+ scientists in the workforce and academic settings to improve gender diversity.
- Congress must allocate funding and resources to streamline and formalize procedures necessary to ensure federal whistleblowers are protected from retaliation so they can report wrongdoing.
- Invest in supporting women of all ages in the workforce at all stages since resiliency is likely proportional to educational attainment.
- Invest in childcare programs and financial support to enable female scientists to continue working in scientific fields.
- Create and promote job-share programs, part-time, flexible work schedules, and continued remote working arrangements.

- Promote work/life balance adjustments by lessening caregiver burdens placed on them as parents and by the COVID-19 pandemic.
- Adopt zero-tolerance for workplace retaliation, sexual harassment, discrimination, and sexual violence.
- Support and grow women leaders by supporting women and men who push for gender equality.
- Make it easier for women to file patents. Create technology transfer offices and start-up innovation events that target and include female scientists.

A recent publication suggested fifteen recommendations to retain female scientists in biomedicine, including many of the items above and additional funding, mentorship, cultural changes, and a framework for women to balance childcare responsibilities and progress to leadership positions (Davis et al., 2022).

FINDING VOICES FOR THE FUTURE

In 2020, a new nationwide network of pediatricians called the American Academy of Pediatrics' Chapter Climate Advocates Program began a voluntary grassroots initiative to raise awareness of the effects of climate change on children's health (Chakradhar, 2020). As discussed in chapter 11, young children are especially vulnerable to the environmental impacts of climate change. In December 2020, for the first time in history, a coroner ruled that climate change caused a nine-year-old girl's death in the United Kingdom. He ruled she died from acute respiratory failure caused by air pollution (Laville, 2020).

The pandemic added additional stress for our youth, who are already worried about the worsening climate crisis. Before the pandemic, a survey found that younger generations were already suffering from increased rates of anxiety and depression since elected officials were not taking the climate crisis seriously enough. More than 60 percent of younger people surveyed said they feel either "very" or "extremely" worried about climate change. More than half said climate change made them feel "afraid, sad, anxious, angry, powerless, helpless, and/or guilty." A sixteen-year-old included in the study said,

"I think it's different for young people. For us, the destruction of the planet is personal."

—(PRUITT-YOUNG, 2021; MARKS ET AL., 2021).

Aaron Bernstein, a pediatrician at Boston Children's Hospital and interim director of the Center for Climate, Health, and the Global Environment at the Harvard T.H. Chan School of Public Health, said, "If only every parent in America knew that climate action was essential to the well-being of their child and family, we would have no political discourse, no debates about the science, no concerns about the course of action" (Chakradhar, 2020).

Young people held walkouts and protests to spur elected officials into climate action. For example, Greta Thunberg, age eighteen, from Sweden, was named *Time Magazine*'s Person of the Year in 2019 when she started a global movement of school strikes calling for climate action. She inspired four million people to join her in a global climate strike on September 20, 2019; hundreds of thousands of teenage Gretas from Lebanon to Liberia skipped school and led climate strikes worldwide (Alter, Haynes, and Worland, 2019).

The more people are informed and actively advocate for climate action and public health protections, the more likely regulators will have to respond to our calls for appropriate action.

WE CAN DO THIS!

There may be a silver lining in the challenges we face.

And, as we emerge and recover from the pandemic, we have a chance to not just return to our old ways but to make the changes necessary to address the structural inequities that limit the professional capacity of female scientists. We have the chance to realign imbalances that will empower women to use their expertise to solve the complex challenges ahead while assigning value to their contributions.

While there's a lot of work to be done, we must each do our part. "We must not think that these efforts are not going to change the world. They benefit society, often unbeknownst to us, for they call forth a goodness which, albeit unseen, inevitably tends to spread" (Francis and Oreskes, 2015). While sometimes things don't change overnight, sometimes the unseen seed is planted by our efforts that, with continued advocacy, inevitably change occurs. For example, while New Jersey acted in 2006, more than ten years later, it still took two years for New Hampshire to enact more robust protections for arsenic in drinking water. But it took a female scientist and curious and supportive legislators to push for the change.

Hopefully, the examples of mighty female scientists throughout this book exemplify how one person can have the power to instigate change. Like Dr. Mona Hanna-Attisha, my hope is that future badass young women will read this and realize they can do this too.

Every step taken is a step forward.

The current political climate threatens to set us back on steps necessary to address climate change. But, when there is the will, there is a way to reduce emissions that are warming the atmosphere. As discussed in chapter 12, Dr. Corinne Le Quéré identified precipitous drops in carbon dioxide levels at the start of the pandemic when the world shut down; this is clear evidence that reducing anthropogenic emissions is an important tool to address climate change.

This COP26 Resolution summed it up nicely: "We join together as women leaders to call on all leaders—women and men—both in government and civil society—to commit to increased and sustained support for women's and girls' climate change initiatives at the national and global levels to achieve sustainable progress toward meeting the challenges of the climate crisis" (Scottish Government and UN Women at COP26, 2021).

I hope that advocating for some of the actions and ideas presented in this book will empower female scientists and encourage more young women to enter and stick with STEM fields. Their talents and perspectives are absolutely vital to answering the myriad challenges we face.

ACKNOWLEDGMENTS

Writing a book is not something I would have anticipated doing. I certainly could not have done it without the support of my family and friends. I want to thank my husband, Mike, and my sons, Justin and Kegan, for their support and help. Also, thank you to my father- and mother-in-law, who have always supported my family and our endeavors. I only wish my mother had lived to read it. I also wish my good friend Renny Cushing were here to read it.

I'd also like the thank the amazing nurses, doctors, and health care workers at Massachusetts General Hospital who helped my family through one of the most stressful and heartbreaking times of our lives.

Thank you Bill Couzens, for the support, guidance, and friendship throughout many years and challenges.

It certainly would not have been possible without the fantastic stories provided by all the wonderful interviewees who graciously contributed their time to my endless questions. Your stories and journeys are truly inspiring and will impact anyone who reads this book. Thank you, thank you, thank you to Dr. Linda Birnbaum, Dr. Mona Hanna-Attisha, Dr. Kyla Bennett, Dr. Elisabeth Bik, Dr. Michelle Fiscus, Ms.

Priya Shukla, Ms. Shanika Amarakoon, Ms. Bonnie Bracey Sutton, Dr. Nawar Shara, Ms. Fiona McEnamy, Dr. Samuel Miller, and Attorney Rob Bilott. Thank you also to the tireless dedication of thousands of scientists and researchers, some of whose stories are mentioned in this book and the many more who are not.

This book would not have been possible without the hours and hours spent by Dr. Mark A. Mastromarino, who provided extensive support and valuable expertise on subject matter guidance throughout the editing process. I'm also eternally grateful to Erica R. de Vries, whose hours spent editing and providing insight regarding women and feminist issues were vital to this book.

This book would not have been possible without all the hard work and dedication from my amazing team from New Degrees Press, the author coaches, and the Book Creator program created by Professor Eric Koester at Georgetown University. I'm so thankful to Michael Biarnes for suggesting it and Dr. Koester's course that helped me learn about the authoring and publishing process. Thanks much to Karina Agbisit, Chuck Oexmann, Linda Berardelli, Tasslyn Magnusson, Venus Bradley, and Ruslan Nabiev. Also, thanks to Jade Reid for promotional video work and the fantastic illustrators like Nikola Tikoski who put my ideas on paper, and Gjorgji Pejkovski and Simona Gjurovska for their amazing cover artwork.

I decided to publish this book with a hybrid publisher, which meant that I would retain creative and intellectual rights. I maintained control over the book's content, artwork, and marketing. To do that, I had to raise funds through a preorder campaign. The outpouring of support received throughout this process was truly inspiring and moving.

Thank you, thank you, thank you to all my friends and family who supported this book and made its publication possible, sight unseen. I am eternally grateful. Thank you!

Mackenzie Murphy, Richard Bednar, Margaret DiTulio, Coeli Hoover, Joyce C Kemp, Celinda Constance Lake, Stephanie Spyvee, Mary Ann Eisner, Barbara McLaughlin, Rebecca McBeath, Dennis Shanahan, Gina Maranto, Patricia Bushway, Angelique Lippmann, Beverly Pietlicki, Mary-Ann McGarry, Jillian Lane, David Watters, Francesca Diggs, Mark Gearreald and Sharon Spickler, Ann Mayer, Caroline French, Tim Josephson, Mark Mattson, Alison Freidlin, Pam Bingham, Kristina Snyder, Michelle Chappell, Claire Karibian, Mary Brennan, John O. Willis, Laurie A McCray, Arvilla Mastromarino, Charles Race, Michael Biarnes, Emily A Zajano, Melinda Vieira, Cyric Riley, Lisa Hix, Suzanne Barton, Beth Nelson, David Vroom, Liz-Anne Platt, Jim Murray, Shannon Jackson, Charlotte I DiLorenzo, Rosemarie L Rung, Lewis Henry, Leslie Kruithof, Douglas Whitbeck, Kris Robertshaw, Pam Ladds, David Meuse, Nicole Fordey, Emily Delikat, Patricia Gingrich, Michael Dowe, Michelle Fiscus, Michael A Edgar, Roger Jones, Chuck Grassie, Holly Grossman, Gail Mitchell, Cristina Drondoe, Mary Beth Raven, Lee Roberts, Patricia Pustell, Melissa Demers, Peter White, Bonnie Chehames, Sue Nastasi, Denise Ward, Tom Irwin, Patricia E. Anderson, Anita Sherrie Klein, William Couzens, Martha Fuller Clark, Brenda Berkal, Mary L. Cady, Eleanor Dunfey-Freiburger and Jim Freiburger, Amy Moore, Dr. Ben Locwin, Elizabeth Edwards-Appell, Katy Henley, Lisa DeMio, Martha Burrill StJean, Kevin Fleming, Cathleen Hodson, Roberta Treece, Robert J. Landman, Debra Merrick, Emily Frazier, Barbara R Bowlus, Kevin Woolley, Kathy Slade, Erica de Vries, Natalie Barefoot, Susan Moniz, Herbert Moyer, Thomas Hourihan, Lesley Pacey, Sheryl Neal, Beatrice Cataldo, Jennifer Cardinal, Ray Madore, Glen Traquair, Chris Evans, Patricia Faubert, Janice Kelble, Linda Rhodes, Karen Steele, Jennifer Brackett Piskovitz, Nancy Martin, Nancy Brady Severn, Candace Moulton, Joshua Lent, Theo Groh, Liz Tentarelli, Liza Draper, Andrea Ernst, Heidi Hanson, Mark W Pitcock, Annie Robbins, Melissa Rigazio, Doris C Brock, Nawar Shara, Alexander Matthew Freid, Mary and John Mitchell, Eric Koester, Melanie Muns, Rachel S DeCicco, Nora Traviss, Deb Cinamon, Mark R Harrison, Eiji Miki, Peter Hoe Burling, Deborah Sillay, Herman Messmer, Kim Loosmann, Amy Webb, Winnie Brinks, Nancy Dowey, John Tuthill, Brenda Bouchard, Peter Miller, Stephane Thornton,

BIBLIOGRAPHY

—

CHAPTER 1: SOUNDING THE ALARM

Alley, Rebecca. "Chemicals found in Cutler Wells." The Ellsworth American, October 29, 2020. https://www.ellsworthamerican. com/maine-news/chemicals-found-in-cutler-wells/.

American Cancer Society. "Risk Factors for Acute Lymphocytic Leukemia (ALL)." 2022. https://www.cancer.org/cancer/ acute-lymphocytic-leukemia/causes-risks-prevention/risk-factors.html.

Bilott, Rob. "The Poison found in Everyone, Even Unborn Babies—and Who is Responsible for It." The Guardian, December 17, 2020. https://www.theguardian.com/commentisfree/2020/dec/17/ dark-waters-pfas-ticking-chemical-time-bomb-in-your-blood.

C8 Science Panel. "The Science Panel Website." Last modified January 22, 2020. http://www.c8sciencepanel.org.

Centers for Disease Control and Prevention. "Cancer Clusters." Last modified May 14, 2019. https://www.cdc.gov/nceh/clusters/about.htm.

Cook, Robert. "Obituary: Lydia Isabelle Valdez." Last modified May 8, 2013. https://patch.com/new-hampshire/portsmouth-nh/obituary-lydia-isabelle-valdez.

Cutler, J. J., Gregg S. Parker, S. Rosen, B. Prenney, R. Healey, and G. G. Caldwell. "Childhood Leukemia in Woburn, Massachusetts." Public Health Reports (Washington, D.C.: 1974) 101, no. 2 (Mar 1986): 201—205. https://pubmed.ncbi.nlm.nih.gov/3083476 https://www.ncbi.nlm.nih.gov/pmc/articles/PMC1477799/.

Ding, Guodong, Rong Shi, Yu Gao, Yan Zhang, Michihiro Kamijima, Kiyoshi Sakai, Guoquan Wang, Chao Feng, and Ying Tian. "Pyrethroid Pesticide Exposure and Risk of Childhood Acute Lymphocytic Leukemia in Shanghai." Environmental Science & Technology 46, no. 24 (November 2012): 13480—13487. doi:10.1021/es303362a. https://doi.org/10.1021/es303362a.

Domagalski, Theresa A. "Contaminated Water and Leukemia in Woburn, MA: The Failings of Civil Action." Organization & Environment 12, no. 3 (September 1999): 332—338. http://www.jstor.org/stable/26161481.

Environmental Working Group. "For decades, the Department of Defense Knew Firefighting Foams with 'forever Chemicals' were Dangerous but Continued their Use." 2018. https://www.ewg.org/dodpfastimeline/.

Foster's Daily Democrat. "Obituary: Samuel G. Thomas." Last modified August 8-11, 2014. https://www.legacy.com/us/obituaries/fosters/name/samuel-thomas-obituary?pid=172020121.

Goodman, Michael, Joshua S. Naiman, Dina Goodman, and Judy S. LaKind. "Cancer Clusters in the USA: What do the Last Twenty Years of State and Federal Investigations Tell Us?" Critical Reviews in Toxicology 42, no. 6 (April 2012): 474—490. doi:10 .3109/10408444.2012.675315. https://doi.org/10.3109/10408444. 2012.675315.

Grandjean, Philippe, Elizabeth W. Andersen, Esben Budtz-Jørgensen, Flemming Nielsen, Kåre Mølbak, Pal Weihe, and Carsten Heilmann. "Serum Vaccine Antibody Concentrations in Children Exposed to Perfluorinated Compounds." JAMA 307, no. 4 (January 2012): 391–397.

Grandjean, Philippe, Clara Amalie, Gade Timmermann, Marie Kruse, Flemming Nielsen, Pernille Just Vinholt, Lasse Boding, Carsten Heilmann, and Kåre Mølbak. "Severity of COVID-19 at elevated exposure to perfluorinated alkylates." PLoS ONE 15, no. 12 (December 2020). doi:https://doi.org/10.1371/ journal.pone.0244815. https://journals.plos.org/plosone/article?id=10.1371/journal.pone.0244815.

Grufferman, S., H. H. Wang, E. R. DeLong, S. Y. Kimm, E. S. Delzell, and J. M. Falletta. "Environmental Factors in the Etiology of Rhabdomyosarcoma in Childhood." Journal of the National Cancer Institute 68, no. 1 (January 1982): 107—113.

Hettmer, Simone, Zhizhong Li, Andrew N. Billin, Frederic G. Barr, D. D. W. Cornelison, Alan R. Ehrlich, Denis C. Guttridge, et al. "Rhabdomyosarcoma: Current Challenges and their Implications for Developing Therapies." Cold Spring Harbor Perspectives in Medicine 4, no. 11 (November 2014): a025650. doi:10.1101/ cshperspect.a025650. https://www.ncbi.nlm.nih.gov/pmc/articles/PMC4208704/.

Hunter, Jasmin. "Putting New Hampshire's Cancer Cluster in Context." portsmouthnh.com, May 11, 2016.

Leigh, Vivian. "Unraveling a Toxic Nightmare: More Wells show 'Forever Chemicals.'" News Center Maine, May 6, 2021. https://www.newscentermaine.com/article/tech/science/environment/pfas/unraveling-a-toxic-nightmare-more-wells-show-forever-chemicals-pfas-in-maine/97-8aeb7dba-9232-443f-b0e5-d1b74a5b3975.

Long, Jennifer. "Family in Seacoast Cancer Cluster Seeks Answers." WGME, March 10, 2016. https://wgme.com/news/local/family-in-seacoast-cancer-cluster-speaks-to-cbs-13.

McMenemy, Jeff. "Cancer Cluster 'it's Terrifying' Rye Mom Talks about Son's Battle with RMS." Portsmouth Herald, March 10, 2016a. https://tarrant.tx.networkofcare.org/kids/news-article-detail.aspx?id=69326.

McMenemy, Jeff. "Pediatric 'Cancer Cluster' Detected." Seacoast Online, February 28, 2016b. https://www.seacoastonline.com/story/news/local/portsmouth-herald/2016/02/28/pediatric-cancer-cluster-detected/32375803007/.

Messmer, Mindi F., Jeffrey Salloway, Nawar Shara, Ben Locwin, Megan W. Harvey, and Nora Traviss. "Risk of Cancer in a Community Exposed to Per- and Poly-Fluoroalkyl Substances." Environmental Health Insights 16 (February 2022): 11786302221076707. doi:10.1177/11786302221076707. https://doi.org/10.1177/11786302221076707.

National Cancer Institute. "Cancer Clusters." 2018. https://www.cancer.gov/about-cancer/causes-prevention/risk/substances/cancer-clusters-fact-sheet.

New Hampshire Department of Health and Human Services. Investigation of Rhabdomyosarcoma (RMS) Cases in the Rye Area. Division of Public Health Services. 2016.

New Hampshire Division of Health and Human Services. New Hampshire Childhood Cancer—January 2009 Issue Brief. Division of Public Health Services. 2009.

Office of Health Statistics and Data Management. New Hampshire, Childhood Cancer, January 2009 — Issue Brief. 2009.

PDQ Pediatric Treatment Editorial Board. Childhood Rhabdomyosarcoma Treatment (PDQ®): Health Professional Version. PDQ Cancer Information Summaries [Internet]. Bethesda (MD), 2021.

Sexton, Adam. "State Holds Meeting on Pediatric Cancer Cluster in Seacoast Area." WMUR, March 15, 2016. https://www.wmur.com/article/state-holds-meeting-on-pediatric-cancer-cluster-in-seacoast-area-1/5209440.

Sunderland, E. M., X. C. Hu, C. Dassuncao, A. K. Tokranov, C. C. Wagner, and J. G. Allen. "A Review of the Pathways of Human Exposure to Poly- and Perfluoroalkyl Substances (PFASs) and Present Understanding of Health Effects." Journal of Exposure Science & Environmental Epidemiology 29, no. 2 2019): 131–147. doi://dx.doi.org/10.1038/s41370-018-0094-1. https://www.ncbi.nlm.nih.gov/pmc/articles/PMC6380916/.

Trimble, Grady. "Parents Concerned about New Hampshire Cancer Cluster." News Center Maine, March 16, 2016. https://www.newscentermaine.com/article/news/local/parents-concerned-about-nh-cancer-cluster/84470193.

U.S. Environmental Protection Agency. "PFAS Master List of PFAS Substances (Version 2)." Last modified August 10, 2021. https://comptox.epa.gov/dashboard/chemical_lists/PFAS-MASTER.

U.S. Environmental Protection Agency. "Superfund Site: Wells G & H Woburn, MA." Last modified February 2, 2022. https://cumulis.epa.gov/supercpad/SiteProfiles/index.cfm?fuseaction=second.Cleanup&id=0100749#bkground.

Zaillian, Scott Rudin, Robert Redford, and Rachel Pfeffer. A Civil Action. North America: Touchstone Pictures, Paramount Pictures Inc, and Wildwood Enterprises. 1998.

Zhang, Qian, Jianan Wang, Chen, Yi Kong, Hong Yan, Jinyan Duan, Chi Wang, Yingjiao Sha, Xinyu Wen, and Chengbin Wang. "Perfluorooctanoic Acid Induces Migration and Invasion and Inhibits Apoptosis through the PI3K/AKT Signaling Pathway in Human Rhabdomyosarcoma Cells." Oncol Rep; Oncology Reports 42, no. 4 (August 2019): 1558—1568. doi:https://doi.org/10.3892/or.2019.7265. https://doi.org/10.3892/or.2019.7265.

CHAPTER 2: TOXIC SOUP

Agency for Toxic Substances and Disease Control. Health Assessment for Coakley Landfill Greenland, Rockingham County, New Hampshire—Addendum. 1992.

Agency for Toxic Substances and Disease Registry. Health Assessment for Coakley Landfill; North Hampton, New Hampshire. 1988.

Carmichael, Lindsey. "PFAS contamination of our water supplies is real and costly." New Hampshire Business Review, January 14, 2019. https://www.nhbr.com/pfas-contamination-of-our-water-supplies-is-real-and-costly/.

Order on Petition for Injunctive Relief Pursuant to Right-To-Know Law RSA 91-A (New Hampshire Superior Court 2018).

Favinger, Larry. "State should Help Pay for Landfill Cleanup." Portsmouth Herald, July 8, 1990.

Karrh, Bruce W., M.D. Ammonium Perflurooctanoate (FC-143) C-8 Compounds. Internal 3M Memorandum, 1981.

McMenemy, Jeff. "Coakley group got millions for work it never did." Seacoast Online, March 3, 2018. https://www.seacoastonline. com/story/news/local/portsmouth-herald/2018/03/03/coakley-group-got-millions-for/13811489007/.

McMenemy, Jeff. "Coakley landfill stirs fear, anger from residents." Seacoast Online, December 18, 2016a. https://www.fosters.com/story/news/2016/12/18/coakley-landfill-stirs-fear-anger-from-residents/23911349007/.

McMenemy, Jeff. "Father who lost son to cancer calls for action." Seacoast Online, November 4, 2016b. https://amp.newsherald. com/amp/24619023007.

Meany, Patricia L. Explanation of Significant Differences Coakley Landfill Superfund Site, North Hampton, New Hampshire. Boston, Massachusetts, 1999.

Messmer et al., v. Coakley Landfill Group. "Mindi Messmer, Robert Renny Cushing, Philip Bean, Henry Marsh, Mike Edgar, & James Splaine v. Coakley Landfill Group and Robert Sullivan, Petition for Injunctive Relief Pursuant to Right-to-Know Law RSA 91-A." State of New Hampshire Superior Court, March 16, 2018. http://mediad.publicbroadcasting.net/p/nhpr/files/201803/messmer_et_al_vs_clg_draft_filed_march_16_2018.pdf.

New Hampshire Division of Public Health Services. Appeal of Eugene Schwartz, M.D. New Hampshire Personnel Appeals Board. 1989.

New Hampshire Division of Health and Human Services. New Hampshire Childhood Cancer—January 2009 Issue Brief. Division of Public Health Services. 2009.

N.H Department of Health and Human Services. Investigation of Rhabdomyosarcoma (RMS) Cases in the Rye Area. Division of Public Health Services. 2016.

New Hampshire Division of Public Health Services. Evaluation of Cancer Incidence and Mortality in North Hampton, New Hampshire, 1980-1986, DPHS Report #88—007. 1988.

Russell, Dick, Sanford Lewis, and Brian Keating. Inconclusive by Design: Waste, Fraud and Abuse in Federal Environmental Health Research. Environmental Health Network and National Toxics Campaign Fund. 1992.

Schreiber, Jason. "Millions at stake in landfill battle." Seacoast Online, July 24, 1998, updated December 15, 2010. https://www.google.com/url?sa=t&rct=j&q=&esrc=s&source=web&c-d=&ved=2ahUKEwi8xZCAv_PoAhVkkeAKHaQKBioQF-noECAIQAQ&url=https%3A%2F%2Fwww.seacoastonline.com%2Farticle%2F19980724%2FNEWS%2F307249996&us-g=AOvVaw3pw2N6GIaXn4SxB77mTvBH.

U.S Environmental Protection Agency. Hearing Re: Superfund Program Coakley Landfill Site North Hampton, New Hampshire. (Massachusetts, 1990).

U.S. Environmental Protection Agency. Potential Hazardous Waste Site, Site Inspection Report, Coakley Landfill, N. Hampton, New Hampshire. (Massachusetts, 1983).

U.S. Environmental Protection Agency — Region I. "Coakley Landfill Group Participation Agreement." (Massachusetts, 1991).

Young, Bob. "Toxic Waste." Seacoast Life Magazine, Fall 1988.

Yu, Wong, Deborah M. Hussey Freeland, and Kari C. Nadeau. "Food Allergy: Immune Mechanisms, Diagnosis and Immunotherapy." Nature Reviews. Immunology 16, no. 12 (December 2016): 751—765. doi:10.1038/nri.2016.111. https://pubmed.ncbi. nlm.nih.gov/27795547 https://www.ncbi.nlm.nih.gov/pmc/articles/PMC5123910/.

CHAPTER 3: RUNNING FOR A CAUSE

Bash, Dana. "How New Hampshire's First Female Senator Moved Off the Sidelines." CNN Politics, August 9, 2017. https://www. cnn.com/2017/06/19/politics/jeanne-shaheen-badass-women-of-washington/index.html.

Keith, Tamara. "Best Way to Get Women to Run for Office? Ask Repeatedly." National Public Radio, May 5, 2014. https://www. npr.org/2014/05/05/309832898/best-way-to-get-women-to-run-for-office-ask-repeatedly.

Lavelle, Marianne. "A Record Number of Scientists are Running for Congress, and they Get Climate Change." Inside Climate News, October 23, 2018. https://insideclimatenews.org/news/23102018/ scientist-congress-house-race-candidate-kopser-casten-luria-climate-change-trump-agenda/.

Maron, Dina Fine. "A Conversation with the Only Scientist in Congress." Scientific American, July 31, 2018.

Messmer, Mindi F., Jeffrey Salloway, Nawar Shara, Ben Locwin, Megan W. Harvey, and Nora Traviss. "Risk of Cancer in a Community Exposed to Per- and Poly-Fluoroalkyl Substances." Environmental Health Insights 16 (February 2022):

11786302221076707. doi:10.1177/11786302221076707. https://doi.org/10.1177/11786302221076707.

National Cancer Institute. "SEER Cancer Statistics Review (CSR) 1975-2016." Last modified April 9, 2020. https://seer.cancer.gov/csr/1975_2016/.

National Conference of State Legislators. "Women Serving in 50 States | 2017." Last modified November 7, 2017. https://www.ncsl.org/legislators-staff/legislators/womens-legislative-network/women-in-state-legislatures-for-2017.aspx.

New Hampshire State Senate. 2018. Regulating Groundwater Pollution Caused by Polluting Emissions in the Air and Relative to Standards for Perfluorinated Chemicals in Drinking Water, Ambient Groundwater, and Surface Water. 2018 sess. (07-10-18).

Prasad, Ritu. "Are Voters Biased Against Women Candidates?" BBC News, September 11, 2019. https://www.bbc.com/news/world-us-canada-49569390.

Sexton, Adam. "State Reps. Review Thousands of Documents on Coakley Landfill." WMUR, March 30, 2018. https://www.wmur.com/article/state-reps-review-thousands-of-documents-on-coakley-landfill/19646381#.

Steinhauser, Paul. "Shea-Porter Says She Won't Seek Re-Election to N.H Congressional Seat." The Concord Monitor, October 6, 2017. https://www.concordmonitor.com/Shea-Porter-not-running-again-2018-12959053.

U.S. Environmental Protection Agency. "PFAS Master List of PFAS Substances (Version 2)." Last modified August 10, 2021. https://comptox.epa.gov/dashboard/chemical_lists/PFASMASTER.

Werft, Meghan. "Each Time a Woman Runs for Office, this is what She's Up Against." Global Citizen, May 25, 2017. https://www.globalcitizen.org/en/content/women-barriers-politics/.

CHAPTER 4: WHEN WOMEN WEAR PANTS

Adducci, Shannon. "The Politics of Power Dressing for Female Elected Officials in 2020 and Beyond." Footwear News, June 5, 2019.

Bain, Marc. "A Brief History of Women's Fight to Wear Pants." Last modified May 8, 2019. https://qz.com/quartzy/1597688/a-brief-history-of-women-in-pants/.

Banchefsky, Sarah, Jacob Westfall, Bernadette Park, and Charles M. Judd. "But You Don't Look Like A Scientist! Women Scientists with Feminine Appearance are Deemed Less Likely to be Scientists." Sex Roles 75, no. 3 (February 2016): 95–109. doi:10.1007/s11199-016-0586-1. https://doi.org/10.1007/s11199-016-0586-1.

Barber, Nigel. "Why Looks Still Matter as Women Gain Power." Psychology Today, July 18, 2018. https://www.psychologytoday.com/us/blog/the-human-beast/201807/why-looks-still-matter-women-gain-power.

BBC News. "Paris Women Finally Allowed to Wear Trousers." BBC News, February 4, 2013.

Blazina, Carrie and Drew Desilver. "A Record Number of Women are Serving in the 117th Congress." Pew Research, January 15, 2021. https://www.pewresearch.org/fact-tank/2021/01/15/a-record-number-of-women-are-serving-in-the-117th-congress/.

Casiano, Louis. "School Tells Girls Not to Show Knees Because it Distracts Male Staff." The New York Post, November 25, 2020.

https://nypost.com/2020/11/25/school-tells-girls-not-to-show-knees-because-it-distracts-male-staff/.

Catalyst. Women of Color in the United States: Quick Take 2022. https://www.catalyst.org/research/women-of-color-in-the-united-states/.

Chrisman-Campbell, Kimberly. "When American Suffragists Tried to 'Wear the Pants'." The Atlantic, June 12, 2019. https://www.theatlantic.com/entertainment/archive/2019/06/american-suffragists-bloomers-pants-history/591484/.

Clemente, Deirdre. "A President in a Pantsuit?" The Conversation, November 7, 2016.

Dean, Madeleine. "This is what Happens to Women when we Say Something, Speak Up." Last modified July 30, 2020. https://twitter.com/RepDean/status/1289308679435464705.

Del Valle, Gaby. "The Real Reason Conservative Critics Love Talking about Alexandria Ocasio-Cortez's Clothes." Vox, November 16, 2018. https://www.vox.com/the-goods/2018/11/16/18099074/alexandria-ocasio-cortez-clothes-eddie-scarry.

DeRoche, Arnaud, and Raul Sanchez. "This French Archaeologist Broke the Law—by Wearing Pants." National Geographic Society, December 18, 2020.

Eskridge, William N., Jr. "Law and the Construction of the Closet: American Regulation of Same-Sex Intimacy, 1880-1946." Iowa Law Review 82, no. 4 (May 1997): 1007–1136. https://openyls.law.yale.edu/bitstream/handle/20.500.13051/3230/Law_and_the_Construction_of_the_Closet__American_Regulation_of_Same_Sex_Intimacy.pdf?sequence=2.

Forster, Eve. "As a Woman in Science, I Need to Conceal My Femininity to be Taken Seriously." Vox, May 4, 2017. https://www.vox.com/first-person/2017/5/4/15536932/women-stem-science-feminism.

Foster, Cassandra. "The Long and Short of Capitol Style." Last modified June 9, 2005. https://www.rollcall.com/2005/06/09/the-long-and-short-of-capitol-style/.

Freidman, Vanessa. "Why we Cover what Politicians Wear." The New York Times, August 17, 2020. https://www.nytimes.com/2020/08/17/style/why-we-cover-what-politicians-wear.html.

Frost, Natasha. "The Women Miners in Pants Who Shocked Victorian Britain." Last modified September 21, 2017. https://www.atlasobscura.com/articles/pit-brow-lasses-women-miners-victorian-britain-pants.

Galdi, Silvia, Anne Maass, and Mara Cadinu. "Objectifying Media: Their Effect on Gender Role Norms and Sexual Harassment of Women." Psychology of Women Quarterly 38, no. 3 (September 2014): 398–413. doi:10.1177/0361684313515185. https://doi.org/10.1177/0361684313515185.

Glakas, Barbara. "Wearing Pants: How Mary Edwards Walker Broke Gender Stereotypes during the Civil War and Beyond." Last modified September 20, 2015. http://historicheroines.org/2015/09/20/wearing-pants-how-mary-edwards-walker-broke-gender-stereotypes-during-the-civil-war-and-beyond/.

Gothreau, Claire. "The Objectification of Women in Politics and Why it Matters." Last modified August 31, 2020. https://cawp.rutgers.edu/blog/objectification-women-politics-and-why-it-matters.

Greenberg, Isabel. "Twitter is Dragging this Tone-Deaf Tweet about Alexandria Ocasio-Cortez's Coat and Jacket." Harpers Bazaar, November 16, 2018. https://www.harpersbazaar.com/culture/politics/a25165778/alexandria-ocasio-cortez-jacket-coat-tweet-memes/.

Job, Zakiyyah. "The Not-so-Straightforward Story of Women and Trousers." Last modified March 17, 2021. https://www.messynessychic.com/2021/03/17/the-not-so-straightforward-story-of-women-and-trousers/.

Kester, Marie. "Two Women Who were Arrested for Wearing Pants, 80 Years Apart." Last modified March 27, 2021. https://historyofyesterday.com/two-women-who-were-arrested-for-wearing-pants-80-years-apart-cf163135c300.

Labour Tribune. "Pit-Bank Girls." Labour Tribune, March 6, 1886.

Lang, Cady. "Here's Why the Women of Congress Wore White for the 2019 State of the Union Address." Time Magazine, February 6, 2019.

Lange, Katie. "Meet Dr. Mary Walker: The Only Female Medal of Honor Recipient." Last modified March 7, 2017. https://www.army.mil/article/183800/meet_dr_mary_walker_the_only_female_medal_of_honor_recipient.

Lavelle, Marianne. "A Record Number of Scientists are Running for Congress, and they Get Climate Change." Inside Climate News, October 23, 2018. https://insideclimatenews.org/news/23102018/scientist-congress-house-race-candidate-kopser-casten-luria-climate-change-trump-agenda/.

Maass, Anne, Mara Cadinu, Gaia Guarnieri, and Annalisa Grasselli. "Sexual Harassment Under Social Identity Threat: The

Computer Harassment Paradigm." Journal of Personality and Social Psychology 85, no. 5 (November 2003): 853–870. https://psycnet.apa.org/record/2003-09138-006.

Mesch, Rachel. 2020. Before Trans: Three Gender Stories from Nineteenth-Century France. Stanford, CA: Stanford University Press.

Micklewright, Nancy. "Şalvar." Last modified July 14, 2021. https://fashionandrace.org/database/salvar/.

National Park Service. "Dr. Mary Edwards Walker." Last modified April 12, 2021. https://www.nps.gov/people/mary-walker.htm.

News Desk. "Arresting Dress: A Timeline of Anti-Cross-Dressing Laws in the United States." PBS News Hour, May 31, 2015. https://www.pbs.org/newshour/nation/arresting-dress-timeline-anti-cross-dressing-laws-u-s.

North, Anna. "America's Sexist Obsession with what Women Politicians Wear, Explained." Vox, December 3, 2018. https://www.vox.com/identities/2018/12/3/18107151/alexandria-ocasio-cortez-eddie-scarry-women-politics.

Oakes, Bradlyn, and John Last. "Women on Arctic Research Mission Told Not to Wear Tight-Fitting Clothing." CBC News, September 28, 2020. https://www.cbc.ca/news/canada/north/mosaic-dress-code-sexism-arctic-research-1.5739547.

Payscale. The State of the Gender Pay Gap in 2021. 2022. https://www.payscale.com/research-and-insights/gender-pay-gap/.

Rothschild, Lauren E. "The Gender Gap in American Politics: How Money in Politics Affects Female Representation." Inquiries Journal 12, no. 10 (2020). http://www.inquiriesjournal.com/articles/1811/the-gender-gap-in-american-politics-how-money-in-politics-affects-female-representation.

Sears, Claire. 2014. Arresting Dress: Cross-Dressing, Law, and Fascination in Nineteenth-Century San Francisco. Durham, NC: Duke University Press.

Silver, Nate. "Gender Pay Gap Tracks with Number of Women in State Legislatures." FiveThirtyEight, April 9, 2014. https://fivethirtyeight.com/features/the-gender-pay-gap-and-womens-representation-in-political-office/.

Smith, Julia K., Miriam Liss, Mindy J. Erchull, Celeste M. Kelly, Kathleen Adragna, and Katlyn Baines. "The Relationship between Sexualized Appearance and Perceptions of Women's Competence and Electability." Sex Roles 79, no. 11 (February 2018): 671–682. doi:10.1007/s11199-018-0898-4. https://doi.org/10.1007/s11199-018-0898-4.

Statista Research Department. "Percent Distribution of Workers Paid Hourly Rates with Earnings at Or Below Minimum Wage in the U.S. 2020, by Full and Part Time Status and Gender." Statista, April 26, 2021. https://www.statista.com/statistics/299318/percent-distribution-of-us-minimum-wage-workers-by-gender-and-working-hours/.

Tagawa, Beth. "When Cross-Dressing was Criminal: Book Documents History of Longtime San Francisco Law." San Francisco State University, December 2014. https://news.sfsu.edu/when-cross-dressing-was-criminal-book-documents-history-longtime-san-francisco-law#:~:text=San%20Francisco%20was%20not%20alone,in%20effect%20until%20July%201974.

Tenure, she wrote. "Dressing for Academia." Tenure, She Wrote, July 15, 2013. https://tenureshewrote.wordpress.com/2013/07/15/dressing-for-academia/.

U.S. Census Bureau. "Quickfacts United States Dashboard." Last modified April 1, 2021. https://www.census.gov/quickfacts/fact/table/US/POP010220.

Vintage Everyday. "Wigan's Pit Brow Lasses: 40 Fascinating Vintage Photos of Women Miners in Pants Who Shocked Victorian Britain." Last modified January 6, 2020. https://vintagenewsdaily.com/wigans-pit-brow-lasses-40-fascinating-vintage-photos-of-women-miners-in-pants-who-shocked-victorian-britain/

CHAPTER 5: FEMALE SCIENCE PIONEERS

Aridas, Rosemarie. "A "Laidy" Geologist: Dr. Katharine Fowler-Billings." Albany County Historical Society, n.d. https://www.wyoachs.com/people/2018/4/15/a-laidy-geologist-dr-katharine-fowler-billings?fbclid=IwAR0N5-zYuR8ex33GZA-3MY-BA3h1ZQrdZGA1dup7nb71Lg2ceY6KQVWgc40E.

Bentley, Callan. "Stepping-Stones, by Katharine Fowler-Billings." AGU Blogosphere, March 30, 2020. https://blogs.agu.org/mountainbeltway/2020/03/30/stepping-stones-by-katharine-fowler-billings/.

Berkshire Museum. "The Matilda Effect: Matilda Joslyn Gage's Forgotten Work." 2022. https://explore.berkshiremuseum.org/digital-archive/she-shapes-history/matilda-josyln-gage.

Brooks, Paul. 1989. The House of Life: Rachel Carson at Work. Boston, Massachusetts: Houghton Mifflin Company.

Carty, Ryan. "Loud and Clear." Last modified June 27, 2012. https://www.sciencehistory.org/distillations/loud-and-clear.

Des Jardins, Julie. "Madame Curie's Passion." Smithsonian Magazine, October 2011.

Dominus, Susan. "Women Scientists were Written Out of History. It's Margaret Rossiter's Lifelong Mission to Fix That." Smithsonian Magazine, October 2019.

Drake, Kimberly. "4 Women Whose Work Won the Nobel Prize for their Male Colleagues." Medical News Today, March 19, 2021. https://www.medicalnewstoday.com/articles/4-women-whose-work-won-the-nobel-prize-for-their-male-supervisors.

Eylott, Marie-Claire. "Mary Anning: The Unsung Hero of Fossil Discovery." 2022. https://www.nhm.ac.uk/discover/mary-anning-unsung-hero.html.

Fahrenthold, David A. "Bill to Honor Rachel Carson on Hold." The Washington Post, May 23, 2007.

Flores, Jessica. "Doctors, Teachers, NASA Astronauts, Mathematicians, Scientists among USA TODAY List of Influential Women." USA Today, August 13, 2020.

Gallucci, Maria. "Farewell to Vera Rubin: Badass Astronomer and Feminist Icon." Last modified December 26, 2016. https://mashable.com/article/vera-rubin-astronomer-feminist.

Geraghty, Karen. "Protecting the Public: Profile of Dr. Frances Oldham Kelsey." Virtual Mentor 3, no. 7 (July 2001): 252–254. doi:10.1001/virtualmentor.2001.3.7.prol1-0107. https://journalofethics.ama-assn.org/article/protecting-public-profile-dr-frances-oldham-kelsey/2001-07.

Gillard, Eric. "NASA Langley's Hall of Honor Calls 18 Researchers to Join Hallowed Ranks." Last modified June 2, 2017. https://www.nasa.gov/feature/langley/nasa-langley-s-hall-of-honor-calls-18-researchers-to-join-hallowed-ranks.

Goodall, Jane. "Dr. Jane Goodall: Being a Woman was Crucial to My Success in a Male-Dominated Field." Time Magazine, March 9, 2018. https://time.com/5192249/jane-goodall-sexism-gender-equality-documentary/.

Grady, Monica. "Is Marie Skłodowska Curie Still a Good Role Model for Female Scientists at 150?" The Conversation, November 7, 2017. https://theconversation.com/is-marie-sklodowska-curie-still-a-good-role-model-for-female-scientists-at-150-87025.

Greicius, Tony. "When Computers were Human." Last modified November 2, 2016. https://www.nasa.gov/feature/jpl/when-computers-were-human.

Griswold, Eliza. "The Wild Life of 'Silent Spring.'" New York Times Magazine, September 23, 2012.

Harrington, Grainne Isobel. "The Woman Who Redefined Man: Jane Goodall's Life of Activism Continues." Irish Times, July 7, 2018. https://www.irishtimes.com/life-and-style/people/the-woman-who-redefined-man-jane-goodall-s-life-of-activism-continues-1.3548371.

Heinecke, Liz. "When Marie Curie was almost Excluded from Winning the Nobel Prize." Last modified February 18, 2021. https://lithub.com/when-marie-curie-was-almost-excluded-from-winning-the-nobel-prize/.

Howell, Elizabeth. "NASA's Real 'Hidden Figures.'" Last modified February 24, 2020. https://www.space.com/35430-real-hidden-figures.html.

Jones, Reed. "Sexism in Science: Was Rosalind Franklin Robbed of a Nobel Prize?" Last modified March 22, 2021. https://lmuthisweek.lmu.edu/2021/03/22/sexism-in-science-was-rosalind-franklin-robbed-of-a-nobel-prize/.

Kamp, Karin. "The Bravery of Rachel Carson." Last modified May 15, 2014. https://billmoyers.com/2014/05/15/how-one-brave-woman-sparked-the-environmental-movement/.

Kroll, Gary. "Rachel Carson's Silent Spring: A Brief History of Ecology as a Subversive Subject." Online Ethics Center. 2002. https://onlineethics.org/cases/rachel-carsons-silent-spring-brief-history-ecology-subversive-subject.

Leach, Camilla. "Religion and Rationality: Quaker Women and Science Education 1790–1850." Journal of the History of Education Society 35, no. 1 (August 2006): 69—90. doi:10.1080/00467600500419919. https://doi.org/10.1080/00467600500419919.

Lear, Linda. 1997. Rachel Carson: Witness for Nature. 1st ed. New York, NY: Henry Holt and Company.

Lee, Jane J. "6 Women Scientists Who Were Snubbed Due to Sexism." National Geographic, May 19, 2013.

Lewis, Jack. "The Birth of EPA." Last modified November 1985. https://archive.epa.gov/epa/aboutepa/birth-epa.html.

Maria Mitchell Association. "About Maria Mitchell." 2022. https://www.mariamitchell.org/about-maria-mitchell.

Marks, Lara. "Professor Esther Lederberg." Last modified December 2015. https://www.whatisbiotechnology.org/index.php/people/summary/Lederberg_Esther.

McFadden, Robert D. "Frances Oldham Kelsey, Who Saved U.S. Babies from Thalidomide, Dies at 101." New York Times, August 7, 2015. https://www.nytimes.com/2015/08/08/science/frances-oldham-kelsey-fda-doctor-who-exposed-danger-of-thalidomide-dies-at-101.html.

Hidden Figures. Directed by Theodore Melfi. 20th Century Fox, 2017.

Michals, Debra, PhD. "Rachel Carson." 2015. https://www.womenshistory.org/education-resources/biographies/rachel-carson.

Narkhede, Roma. "Quaker History: Maria Mitchell, the First Female Astronomer in the USA." Last modified March 11, 2020. https://www.pym.org/quaker-history-maria-mitchell-the-first-female-astronomer-in-the-usa/.

National Geographic Society. "Women of NASA." Last modified March 2, 2020. https://www.nationalgeographic.org/article/women-nasa/.

National Park Service. "Dr. Mary Edwards Walker." Last modified April 12, 2021. https://www.nps.gov/people/mary-walker.htm.

Newman, Cathy. "The Forgotten Fossil Hunter Who Transformed Britain's Jurassic Coast." National Geographic, March 29, 2021.

NobelPrize.org. "Nobel Prize Awarded Women." Last modified January 14, 2022. https://www.nobelprize.org/prizes/lists/nobel-prize-awarded-women/.

Pasachoff, Naomi. "Madame Curie and the Science of Radioactivity." 2000. https://history.aip.org/exhibits/curie/scandal1.htm.

Proudfoot, Ben. "She Changed Astronomy Forever. He Won the Nobel Prize for it." New York Times, July 27, 2021. https://www.nytimes.com/2021/07/27/opinion/pulsars-jocelyn-bell-burnell-astronomy.html.

Soter, Steven, and Neil deGrasse Tyson. "Vera Rubin and Dark Matter." 2000. https://www.amnh.org/learn-teach/curriculum-collections/cosmic-horizons-book/vera-rubin-dark-matter.

Springfield Union, The. "Blonde Finds Chimps Look Down on Humans." The Springfield Union, February 28, 1964. https://www.rarenewspapers.com/view/661624?imagelist=1#full-images.

Stampler, Laura. "Jane Goodall Talks Women in Science." Huffpost, December 6, 2017. https://www.huffpost.com/entry/jane-goodall-women-science_n_982793.

Steinmetz, Katy. "Esther Lederberg and Her Husband were both Trailblazing Scientists. Why have More People Heard of Him?" Time Magazine, April 11, 2019.

Stoll, Mark. "Rachel Carson's Silent Spring, a Book that Changed the World." Environment & Society Portal, updated February 6, 2020. doi:https://doi.org/10.5282/rcc/8842. https://www.environmentandsociety.org/exhibitions/rachel-carsons-silent-spring.

The Nobel Foundation. "Nobel Prize Facts." 2022. https://www.nobelprize.org/prizes/facts/nobel-prize-facts/.

Trombetta, Mark. "Madame Maria Sklodowska-Curie—Brilliant Scientist, Humanitarian, Humble Hero: Poland's Gift to the World." Journal of Contemporary Brachytherapy 6, no. 3 (October 2014): 297–299. doi:10.5114/jcb.2014.45133. https://pubmed.ncbi.nlm.nih.gov/25337133 https://www.ncbi.nlm.nih.gov/pmc/articles/PMC4200180/.

Van der Does, Louise Q., and Rita James Simon. 1999. Renaissance Women in Science. Illustrated ed. University of Michigan: University Press of America.

Walsh, Fergus. "The most Important Photo Ever Taken?" BBC News, May 16, 2012. www.bbc.com/news/health-18041884.

Watson, J. D., and F. H. Crick. "Molecular Structure of Nucleic Acids: A Structure for Deoxyribose Nucleic Acid." Nature 171, no. 4356 (April 1953): 737–738. doi:10.1038/171737a0. https://doi.org/10.1038/171737a0.

Wei-Haas, Maya. "The True Story of 'Hidden Figures.'" Smithsonian Magazine, September 8, 2016.

Wu, Katherine J. "Decades After Being Passed Over for A Nobel, Jocelyn Bell Burnell Gets Her Due." Smithsonian Magazine, September 10, 2018.

Zielinski, Sarah. "The Rise and Fall and Rise of the Chemistry Set." Smithsonian Magazine, October 10, 2012. https://www.smithsonianmag.com/science-nature/the-rise-and-fall-and-rise-of-the-chemistry-set-70359831/

CHAPTER 6: NOBODY LIKES A SNITCH

Abritis, Alison, Marcus, Adam, and Ivan Oransky. "The Retraction Watch Leaderboard." 2022. https://retractionwatch.com/the-retraction-watch-leaderboard/.

Alms, Natalie. "MSPB Passes Five-Year Mark without a Quorum." Fcw, January 11, 2022. https://fcw.com/workforce/2022/01/mspb-passes-five-year-mark-without-quorum/360604/.

Besançon, Lonni, Alexander Samuel, Thibault Sana, Mathieu E. Rebeaud, Anthony Guihur, Marc Robinson-Rechavi, Nicolas Le Berre, et al. Open Letter: Scientists Stand Up to Protect Academic Whistleblowers and Post-Publication Peer Review. OSF Preprints, 2021.

Bik, Elisabeth. "Thoughts on the Gautret et al. Paper about Hydroxychloroquine and Azithromycin Treatment of COVID-19 Infections." Last modified March 24, 2020. https://scienceintegritydigest.com/2020/03/24/thoughts-on-the-gautret-et-al-paper-about-hydroxychloroquine-and-azithromycin-treatment-of-covid-19-infections/.

Blackman, Matthew, and Nick Dall. "High-Stakes Heroes: Some of SA's Bravest Whistle-Blowers have been Women." Financial Mail, September 2, 2021. https://www.businesslive.co.za/fm/features/2021-09-02-high-stakes-heroes-sas-bravest-whistle-blowers-have-been-women/.

Booker, Brakkton, Emily Birnbaum, and Leah Nylen. "Whistleblowing Doesn't Pay for Women of Color." Politico, October 12, 2021. https://www.politico.com/newsletters/the-recast/2021/10/12/whistleblowing-women-of-color-facebook-testimony-494670.

Bur, Jessie. "How Merit Board Nominees Plan to Address the Ever-Growing Backlog." Federal Times, September 22, 2021. https://www.federaltimes.com/management/leadership/2021/09/22/how-merit-board-nominees-plan-to-address-the-ever-growing-backlog/.

Davey, Melissa. "World Expert in Scientific Misconduct Faces Legal Action for Challenging Integrity of Hydroxychloroquine Study." The Guardian, May 22, 2021. https://www.theguardian.com/science/2021/may/22/world-expert-in-scientific-misconduct-faces-legal-action-for-challenging-integrity-of-hydroxychloroquine-study.

Devlin, Hannah. "Misinformation Fueled by 'Tsunami' of Poor." The Guardian, December 1, 2021. https://www.theguardian.

com/science/2021/dec/01/misinformation-fuelled-by-tsuna-mi-of-poor-research-says-science-prize-winner.

Facher, Lev. "FDA Revokes Emergency use Ruling for Hydroxy-chloroquine, the Drug Touted by Trump as a Covid-19 Therapy." Stat News, June 15, 2020. https://www.statnews.com/2020/06/15/fda-revokes-hydroxychloroquine/.

France 24. "France Revokes Decree Authorising use of Hydroxychlo-roquine to Treat Covid-19." France 24 with Reuters, May 27, 2020. https://www.france24.com/en/20200527-france-revokes-de-cree-authorising-use-of-hydroxychloroquine-to-treat-covid-19.

Government Accountability Project. "Women Whistleblowers in the Trump Era: A Celebration of Women Who Refused to be Silenced." 2022. https://whistleblower.org/blog/women-whis-tleblowers-in-the-trump-era-a-celebration-of-women-who-re-fused-to-be-silenced-part-1/.

Jonas, Michael. "This Whistleblower Knows how to Get Agencies' Attention." Commonwealth Magazine, Fall 2003.

Kindelan, Katie. "Dr. Jill Biden Responds After Op-Ed Called for Her to Drop 'doctor' from Name." ABC News, December 18, 2020. https://abcnews.go.com/GMA/News/dr-jill-biden-responds-op-ed-called-drop/story?id=74797472.

Lee, Stephanie M. "A Data Sleuth Challenged A Powerful COVID Scientist. Then He Came After Her." BuzzFeed News, Octo-ber 18, 2021. https://www.buzzfeednews.com/article/stepha-niemlee/elisabeth-bik-didier-raoult-hydroxychloroquine-study.

Lerner, Sharon. "EPA Officials Exposed Whistleblowers Three Minutes After Receiving Confidential Complaint." The Intercept, September 30, 2021. https://theintercept.com/2021/09/30/epa-whistleblowers-exposed/.

Lerner, Sharon. "Leaked Audio shows Pressure to Overrule Scientists in "Hair-on-Fire" Cases." The Intercept, August 4, 2021. https://theintercept.com/2021/08/04/epa-hair-on-fire-chemicals-leaked-audio/.

Lerner, Sharon. "New Evidence of Corruption at EPA Chemicals Division." The Intercept, September 18, 2021. https://theintercept.com/2021/09/18/epa-corruption-harmful-chemicals-testing/.

Lerner, Sharon. "Whistleblowers Expose Corruption in EPA Chemical Safety Office." The Intercept, July 2, 2021. https://theintercept.com/2021/07/02/epa-chemical-safety-corruption-whistleblowers/.

Miceli, Marcia P., and Janet P. Near. 1992. Blowing the Whistle: The Organization & Legal Implications for Companies and Employees. New York: Lexington Books.

National Whistleblower Center. "FAQ: Whistleblower Protection Act." 2022. https://www.whistleblowers.org/faq/whistleblower-protection-act-faq/#:~:text=The%20Whistleblower%20Protection%20Act%20protects,and%20specific%20danger%20to%20public.

NH Science and Public Health, Directed by. "Episode 5: Science Protector, Dr. Elisabeth Bik." January 18, 2022. Ms Information. Podcast, MP3 audio, 42:49.

Noack, Rick. "French Scientist Who Promoted One of Trump's Favorite Coronavirus Cures Set to be Replaced." The Washington Post, September 17, 2021. https://www.washingtonpost.com/

world/europe/didier-raoult-hydroxychloroquine/2021/09/17/
a56c5bd4-1574-11ec-a019-cb193b28aa73_story.html.

Office of Research Integrity. Consequences of Whistleblowing
for the Whistleblower in Misconduct in Science Cases. 1995.

Platt, Rutherford H., and James M. Kendra. "The Sears Island
Saga: Law in Search of Geography." Economic Geography 74,
(March 1998): 46–61. doi:10.2307/144303. http://www.jstor.org/
stable/144303.

Rehg, Michael T., Marcia P. Miceli, Janet P. Near, and James R. Van
Scotter. "Antecedents and Outcomes of Retaliation Against
Whistleblowers: Gender Differences and Power Relationships." Organization Science 19, no. 2 (March 2008): 221—240.
doi:10.1287/orsc.1070.0310. https://doi.org/10.1287/orsc.1070.0310.

Scientific Integrity Digest. "Concerns about Marseille's IHUMI/
AMU Papers—Part 1." Last modified June 2, 2021. https://scien-
ceintegritydigest.com/2021/06/02/concerns-about-marseilles-
ihumi-amu-papers-part-1/.

Shrader-Frechette, K. S. 2000. Ethics of Scientific Research. United States: Rowman & Littlefield Publishers.

Solender, Andrew. "All the Times Trump has Promoted Hydroxychloroquine." Forbes, May 22, 2020.

Temin, Tom. "Despite Laws, Federal Whistleblowers Still Face
Problems." February 17, 2020. Federal News Network.

U.S. Department of Transportation Federal Highway Administration. "Appendix E—Sears Island/Mack Point." Last modified March 23, 2020. https://ops.fhwa.dot.gov/freight/freight_
analysis/env_factors/env_fact_app_e1.htm.

U.S. Environmental Protection Agency. "John DeVillars Stepping Down as Administrator of EPA's New England Office." November 9, 1999. https://archive.epa.gov/epapages/newsroom_archive/newsreleases/88452aeb1480f52a852574bf006578ae.html.

U.S. Government Accounting Office. Whistleblower Protection—Reasons for Whistleblower Complaints. 1993.

U.S. Merit Systems Protection Board. Whistleblowing in the Federal Government: An Update. 1993.

Vulliamy, Ed. "The Woman Who Took on a Giant." The Observer (1901- 2003), January 27, 2002. https://search.proquest.com/docview/478272985.

West, Jonathan P., and James S. Bowman. "Whistleblowing Policies in American States: A Nationwide Analysis." The American Review of Public Administration 50, no. 2 (February 2020): 119—132. doi:10.1177/0275074019885629. https://doi.org/10.1177/0275074019885629.

CHAPTER 7: WHEN WOMEN LEAD

Adamczyk, Alicia. "Why Women Talk Less than Men at Work." Money, August 12, 2016. https://money.com/men-interrupt-talk-more/.

Associated Press, The. "Doctors Urge Flint to Stop using Water from Flint River." The Associated Press, September 28, 2015. https://www.crainsdetroit.com/article/20150928/NEWS01/150929872/doctors-urge-flint-to-stop-using-water-from-flint-river.

Associated Press, The. "Judge OKs $626 Million Settlement in Flint Water Litigation." Politico, November 10, 2021. https://www.politico.com/news/2021/11/10/flint-water-lead-lawsuit-520747.

Bear, Julia B., and Anita Williams Woolley. "The Role of Gender in Team Collaboration and Performance." Interdisciplinary Science Review 36, no. 2 (November 2011): 146–153. doi:10.11 79/030801811X13013181961473. https://doi.org/10.1179/03080181 1X13013181961473.

Birnbaum, Linda S. "When Environmental Chemicals Act Like Uncontrolled Medicine." Trends in Endocrinology and Metabolism: TEM 24, no. 7 (May 2013): 321–323. doi:10.1016/j. tem.2012.12.005. https://pubmed.ncbi.nlm.nih.gov/23660158 https://www.ncbi.nlm.nih.gov/pmc/articles/PMC6338420/.

Bock, Eric. "Pediatrician Who Uncovered Flint Water Crisis Recounts Experience." NIH Record73, no. 9 (April 30, 2021). https:// nihrecord.nih.gov/sites/recordNIH/files/pdf/2021/NIH-Record-2021-04-30.pdf.

Campbell, Lesley G., Siya Mehtani, Mary E. Dozier, and Janice Rinehart. "Gender-Heterogeneous Working Groups Produce Higher Quality Science." PLoS One 8, no. 10:e79147 (October 2013). doi:https://doi.org/10.1371/journal.pone.0079147. https:// journals.plos.org/plosone/article/metrics?id=10.1371/journal. pone.0079147#citedHeader.

Carroll, Nicole. "Lead was Poisoning the Water in Flint, Mich. Dr. Mona Hanna-Attisha Put Her Reputation on the Line to Prove It." USA Today, August 11, 2020. https://www.usatoday.com/ in-depth/life/women-of-the-century/2020/08/11/19th-amendment-flint-water-crisis-elevated-dr-mona-hanna-attisha/5535823002/.

Childhood Lead Poisoning Prevention. "Flint Lead Exposure Registry." Last modified November 3, 2021. https://www.cdc.gov/ nceh/lead/programs/flint-registry.htm.

Cooper, Marianne. "Do You Like Me?" Last modified April 19, 2016. https://www.leagueofwomeningovernment.org/2016/04/guest-blogger-marianne-cooper-on-women-leaders-and-likability/#:~:text=Women%20are%20expected%20to%20be,how%20she%20%E2%80%9Cshould%E2%80%9D%20behave.

Cornwall, Warren. "Now Retired, Top U.S. Environmental Scientist Feels Free to Speak Her Mind." Science, October 17, 2019. https://www.science.org/content/article/now-retired-top-us-environmental-scientist-feels-free-speak-her-mind.

Cox News Service. "Six Unearthed Bodies Yield Clues to 1918 Spanish Influenza Outbreak; Frozen Corpses found in Norwegian Arctic Help Scientists Study Virus." The Baltimore Sun, November 18, 1999. https://www.baltimoresun.com/news/bs-xpm-1999-11-18-9911180290-story.html.

Del Toral, Miguel A. High Lead Levels in Flint, Michigan—Interim Report. 2015.

DiNisio, A., I. Sabovic, U. Valente, S. Tescari, M. S. Rocca, D. Guidolin, S. Dall'Acqua, et al. "Endocrine Disruption of Androgenic Activity by Perfluoroalkyl Substances: Clinical and Experimental Evidence." Journal of Clinical Endocrinology and Metabolism 104, no. 4 (November 2018): 1259–1271. doi://dx.doi.org/10.1210/jc.2018-01855.

Fonger, Ron. "General Motors Shutting Off Flint River Water at Engine Plant Over Corrosion Worries." MLive, October 13, 2014a. https://www.mlive.com/news/flint/2014/10/general_motors_wont_use_flint.html#incart_river.

Fonger, Ron. "GM's Decision to Stop using Flint River Water Will Cost Flint $400,000 Per Year." MLive, October 14, 2014b. https://

www.mlive.com/news/flint/2014/10/gms_decision_to_stop_using_fli.html.

Fonger, Ron. "USA Today Makes Dr. Mona One of its 100 Women of the Century." MLive, August 11, 2020. https://www.mlive.com/news/flint/2020/08/usa-today-makes-dr-mona-one-of-its-100-women-of-the-century.html.

Gerstein, Terri. "Forced Arbitration in Workplace Sexual Assault Cases is Ending. but what about Other Disputes." NBC News, February 11, 2022. https://www.nbcnews.com/think/opinion/forced-arbitration-workplace-sexual-assault-cases-ending-what-about-other-ncna1288968.

Gewin, Virginia. "Why Joe Biden's Bid to Restore Scientific Integrity Matters." Nature, January 17, 2022. https://www.nature.com/articles/d41586-022-00105-7.

Gross, Liza, and Linda Birnbaum. "Regulating Toxic Chemicals for Public and Environmental Health." PLoS Bio 15, no. 12 (December 2017). doi:https://doi.org/10.1371/journal.pbio.2004814. https://journals.plos.org/plosbiology/article?id=10.1371/journal.pbio.2004814.

Hanna-Attisha, Mona. 2018. "What the Eyes Don't See." First ed. New York: One World, an imprint of Random House.

Ibarra, Herminia, Robin J. Ely, and Deborah M. Kolb. "Women Rising: The Unseen Barriers." Harvard Business Review, September 2013. https://hbr.org/2013/09/women-rising-the-unseen-barriers.

Jordan, Douglas. "The Deadliest Flu: The Complete Story of the Discovery and Reconstruction of the 1918 Pandemic Virus."

CDC Influenza (Flu), December 17, 2019. https://www.cdc. gov/flu/pandemic-resources/reconstruction-1918-virus.html.

Krings, Amy, Dana Kornberg, and Erin Lane. "Organizing Under Austerity: How Residents' Concerns Became the Flint Water Crisis." Critical Sociology 45, no. 4–5 2019): 583–597. doi:10.1177/0896920518757053. https://doi.org/10.1177/0896920518757053.

McKeague, Paul. "The Real Virus: Big Egos and Duplicity." The Globe and Mail, May 24, 2003. https://www.theglobeandmail. com/arts/the-real-virus-big-egos-and-duplicity/article1161780/.

McKenna, Maryn. "Canada's First (and Female) Science Minister is a Badass." National Geographic, November 5, 2015.

Morris, Jim, and Chris Hamby. "Industry Vs. Government Science." Salon, July 30, 2013. https://www.salon.com/2013/07/30/ industry_vs_government_science/.

Moss-Racusin, Corinne, John F. Dovidio, Victoria L. Brescoll, Mark J. Graham, and Jo Handelsman. "Science Faculty's Subtle Gender Biases Favor Male Students." Proceedings of the National Academy of Sciences of the United States of America 109, no. 41 (October 2012): 16474. doi:10.1073/pnas.1211286109. http:// www.pnas.org/content/109/41/16474.abstract.

Nelson, Libby. "Why President Obama just Drank the Water in Flint." Vox, May 4, 2016. https://www.vox.com/2016/5/4/11591894/ obama-flint-water.

Oxford, Esther. "Secrets of the Grave." Independent, September 26, 1998. https://www.independent.co.uk/arts-entertainment/ secrets-of-the-grave-1200930.html.

Ratcliffe, Rebecca. "Nobel Scientist Tim Hunt: Female Scientists Cause Trouble for Men in Labs." The Guardian, June 10, 2015. https://www.theguardian.com/uk-news/2015/jun/10/nobel-scientist-tim-hunt-female-scientists-cause-trouble-for-men-in-labs.

Rehg, Michael T., Marcia P. Miceli, Janet P. Near, and James R. Van Scotter. "Antecedents and Outcomes of Retaliation Against Whistleblowers: Gender Differences and Power Relationships." Organization Science 19, no. 2 (March 2008): 221–240. doi:10.1287/orsc.1070.0310. https://doi.org/10.1287/orsc.1070.0310.

Senz, Kristen. "Lack of Female Scientists Means Fewer Medical Treatments for Women." Harvard Business School, Working Knowledge, February 22, 2022. https://hbswk.hbs.edu/item/lack-of-female-scientists-means-fewer-medical-treatments-for-womenShukla, Priya, and Sarah E. Myhre. "Scientific Service—for Culture and Community." December 8, 2016.

Snyder, Kieran. "How to Get Ahead as a Woman in Tech: Interrupt Men." Slate, July 23, 2014. https://slate.com/human-interest/2014/07/study-men-interrupt-women-more-in-tech-workplaces-but-high-ranking-women-learn-to-interrupt.html.

Thomas-Hunt, Melissa, and Katherine W. Phillips. "When what You Know is Not enough: Expertise and Gender Dynamics in Task Groups." Personality and Social Psychology Bulletin 30, no. 12 (December 2004): 1585–1598. doi:10.1177/0146167204271186. https://doi.org/10.1177/0146167204271186.

Trafton, Anne. "Research Reveals a Gender Gap in the Nation's Biology Labs." MIT News Office, June 30, 2014. https://news.mit.edu/2014/research-reveals-gender-gap-nations-biology-labs-0630.

Zippia. "Scuba Diver Demographics and Statistics in the US." 2022. https://www.zippia.com/scuba-diver-jobs/demographics/.

CHAPTER 8: BUILDING THE BENCH

12 Women Scholars. "A Disturbing Pattern." Last modified August 27, 2021. https://www.insidehighered.com/advice/2021/08/27/entrenched-inequity-not-appropriately-citing-scholarship-women-and-people-color.

Blake-Beard, Stacy, Melissa L. Bayne, Faye J. Crosby, and Carol B. Muller. "Matching by Race and Gender in Mentoring Relationships: Keeping our Eyes on the Prize." Journal of Social Issues 67, no. 3 2011): 622—643. doi:https://doi.org/10.1111/j.1540-4560.2011.01717.x. https://doi.org/10.1111/j.1540-4560.2011.01717.x.

Chatterjee, Paula, and Rachel M. Werner. "Gender Disparity in Citations in High-Impact Journal Articles." JAMA Network Open 4, no. 7 (July 2021): e2114509. doi:10.1001/jamanetworkopen.2021.14509. https://doi.org/10.1001/jamanetworkopen.2021.14509.

Dennehy, Tara C., and Nilanjana Dasgupta. "Female Peer Mentors Early in College Increase Women's Positive Academic Experiences and Retention in Engineering." Proceedings of the National Academy of Sciences of the United States of America 114, no. 23 (June 2017): 59–64. doi:10.1073/pnas.1613117114. http://www.pnas.org/content/114/23/5964.abstract.

Dotson, Bryan. "Women as Authors in the Pharmacy Literature: 1989–2009." American Journal of Health-System Pharmacy 68, no. 18 (September 2011): 1736—1739. doi:10.2146/ajhp100597. https://doi.org/10.2146/ajhp100597.

Filardo, Giovanni, Briget da Graca, Danielle M. Sass, Benjamin D. Pollock, Emma B. Smith, and Melissa Ashley-Marie Martinez. "Trends and Comparison of Female First Authorship in High Impact Medical Journals: Observational Study (1994-2014)." BMJ 352 (March 2016): i847. doi:10.1136/bmj.i847. http://www.bmj.com/content/352/bmj.i847.abstract.

Gould, Julie. "How COVID-19 Changed Scientific Mentoring." September 21, 2021a. Nature Careers.

Grunspan, Daniel Z., Sarah L. Eddy, Sara E. Brownell, Benjamin L. Wiggins, Alison J. Crowe, and Steven M. Goodreau. "Males Under-Estimate Academic Performance of Their Female Peers in Undergraduate Biology Classrooms." PLoS ONE 11, no. 2 (February 10, 2016): e0148405. doi:https://doi.org/10.1371/journal.pone.0148405.

Huckins, Grace. "As More Women Enter Science, It's Time to Redefine Mentorship." Wired, February 11, 2021. https://www.wired.com/story/as-more-women-enter-science-its-time-to-redefine-mentorship/.

Jeffs, Nina. "Why Women's Leadership is Key to Climate Action." China Dialogue, January 18, 2022. https://chinadialogue.net/en/climate/why-womens-leadership-is-key-to-climate-action/.

Khan, Amina. "By Age 6, Girls are Less Likely than Boys to Think that they can be Brilliant, Study Shows." Los Angeles Times, January 26, 2017. https://www.latimes.com/science/sciencenow/la-sci-sn-girls-boys-brilliant-20170126-story.html.

Makarova, Elena, Belinda Aeschlimann, and Walter Herzog. "The Gender Gap in STEM Fields: The Impact of the Gender Stereotype of Math and Science on Secondary Students' Career Aspirations." Frontiers in Education 4,(July 2019). https://www.frontiersin.org/article/10.3389/feduc.2019.00060.

McLaughlin, Catherine. "Mentoring: What is it? How Do We Do It and How Do We Get More of It?" Health Services Research 45, no. 3 (June 2010): 871—884. doi:10.1111/j.1475-6773.2010.01090.x. https://pubmed.ncbi.nlm.nih.gov/20337731 https://www.ncbi.nlm.nih.gov/pmc/articles/PMC2875765/.

Ouyang, David, Robert A. Harrington, and Fatima Rodriguez. "Association between Female Corresponding Authors and Female Co-Authors in Top Contemporary Cardiovascular Medicine Journals." Circulation 139, no. 8 (February 2019): 1127-1129. doi:10.1161/circulationaha.118.037763. https://doi.org/10.1161/CIRCULATIONAHA.118.037763.

Reardon, Sara. "Fewer Citations for Female Authors of Medical Research." Nature Career News, July 29, 2021.

Roberts, Julia Link. "Parents can be Mentors, Too!" Gifted Child Today Magazine 15, no. 3 (May 1992): 36-38. doi:10.1177/107621759201500310. https://doi.org/10.1177/107621759201500310.

Scheinert, Rachel. "The Science of Mentoring Women in Science—Judith Walters: Mentor Extraordinaire." The NIH Catalyst 23, no. 2 (March–April 2015). https://irp.nih.gov/catalyst/v23i2/the-science-of-mentoring-women-in-science.

Schwartz, Sarah E. O., Sarah R. Lowe, and Jean E. Rhodes. "Mentoring Relationships and Adolescent Self-Esteem." The Prevention Researcher 19, no. 2 (April 2012): 17–20. https://pubmed.ncbi.nlm.nih.gov/24376310 https://www.ncbi.nlm.nih.gov/pmc/articles/PMC3873158/.

CHAPTER 9: SCIENCE MOMS

AAUW. "Fast Facts: Women Working in Academia." Last modified Accessed February 11, 2022. https://www.aauw.org/resources/article/fast-facts-academia/.

Almeda, Florence. "Covid-19 Leads to Global Rise in Unplanned Pregnancy." Nova, September 20, 2021. https://www.pbs.org/wgbh/nova/article/unintended-pregnancy-contraceptive-disruption-covid-pandemic/.

Barroso, Amanda, and Amanda Brown. "Gender Pay Gap in U.S. Held Steady in 2020." Pew Research Center, May 25, 2021. https://www.pewresearch.org/fact-tank/2021/05/25/gender-pay-gap-facts/.

Budig, Michelle J. "The Fatherhood Bonus and the Motherhood Penalty: Parenthood and the Gender Gap in Pay." Third Way, September 2, 2014. https://www.thirdway.org/report/the-fatherhood-bonus-and-the-motherhood-penalty-parenthood-and-the-gender-gap-in-pay.

Cech, Erin A., and Mary Blair-Loy. "The Changing Career Trajectories of New Parents in STEM." Proceedings of the National Academy of Sciences 116, no. 10 (January 2019): 4182-4187. https://www.ncbi.nlm.nih.gov/pmc/articles/PMC6919552/.

Corbett, Christianne, and Catherine Hill. "Solving the Equation—The Variables for Women's Success in Engineering and Computing." AAUW (American Association of University Women). 2015.

Correll, Shelley J., Stephen Benard, and In Paik. "Getting a Job: Is There a Motherhood Penalty?" American Journal of Sociology

112, no. 5 (March 2007): 1297–1339. doi:10.1086/511799. https://doi.org/10.1086/511799.

Dunn, Andrew. "Number of Female Biotech CEOs Remains 'Shockingly Low,' Putting Spotlight on BIO." BiopharmaDive, July 31, 2019. https://www.biopharmadive.com/news/female-biotech-ceos-bio-efforts-diversity-goals/558604/.

Elliott, Kate H. "The Fatherhood Bonus and the Motherhood Penalty." Augsburg Now, November 16, 2017. https://www.augsburg.edu/now/2017/11/16/the-fatherhood-bonus-and-the-motherhood-penalty/.

Ferrante, Mary Beth. "Before Breaking the Glass Ceiling, Women must Climb the Maternal Wall." Forbes, October 31, 2019. https://www.forbes.com/sites/marybethferrante/2018/10/31/before-breaking-the-glass-ceiling-women-must-climb-the-maternal-wall/?sh=44d031aec519.

Hall, William M., Toni Schmader, and Elizabeth Croft. "Engineering Exchanges: Daily Social Identity Threat Predicts Burnout among Female Engineers." Social Psychological and Personality Science 6, no. 5 (February 2015): 528—534. doi:https://doi.org/10.1177/1948550615572637. https://psycnet.apa.org/record/2015-25177-007.

Heidt, Amanda. "Push to Address Long-Standing Challenges for Parents in STEM." The Scientist, July 21, 2021. https://www.the-scientist.com/careers/push-to-address-long-standing-challenges-for-parents-in-stemm-68998.

Jones, Rachel K., Elizabeth Witwer, and Jenna Jerman. "Abortion Incidence and Service Availability in the United States, 2017." Guttmacher Institute. 2019.

Kuehn, Bridget M. "Scientist and Parent: Planning during Pregnancy." eLife, May 7, 2019. https://elifesciences.org/articles/47985.

Madowitz, Michael, Alex Rowell, and Katie Hamm. "Calculating the Hidden Cost of Interrupting a Career for Child Care." 2016.

Monosson, Emily. 2008. "Motherhood, the Elephant in the Laboratory." Ithaca, N.Y.: Cornell University Press.

Mordock, Jeff. "C8 Suspected in Birth Defects: One Woman's Story." Delaware Online, April 2, 2016. https://www.delawareonline.com/story/news/2016/04/02/c8-suspected-birth-defects-one-womans-story/81473242/.

Ogden, Lesley Evans. "Working Mothers Face a 'wall' of Bias—but there are Ways to Push Back." Science, April 10, 2019. https://www.science.org/content/article/working-mothers-face-wall-bias-there-are-ways-push-back.

Paquette, Danielle, and Peyton M. Craighill. "The Surprising Number of Parents Scaling Back at Work to Care for Kids." The Washington Post, August 6, 2015. https://www.washingtonpost.com/business/economy/the-surprising-number-of-moms-and-dads-scaling-back-at-work-to-care-for-their-kids/2015/08/06/c7134c50-3ab7-11e5-b3ac-8a79bc44e5e2_story.html.

Potter, Joseph E., Amanda Jean Stevenson, Kate Coleman-Minahan, Kristine Hopkins, Kari White, Sarah E. Baum, and Daniel Grossman. "Challenging Unintended Pregnancy as an Indicator of Reproductive Autonomy." Contraception 100, no. 1 (March 2019): 1-4. doi:10.1016/j.contraception.2019.02.005. https://pubmed.ncbi.nlm.nih.gov/30851238 https://www.ncbi.nlm.nih.gov/pmc/articles/PMC6919552/.

Powell, Kendall. "The Parenting Penalties Faced by Scientist Mothers." Nature, July 20, 2021. https://www.nature.com/articles/d41586-021-01993-x.

Pregnant Scholar, The. "Title IX Basics." 2021. https://thepregnantscholar.org/.

Rosenwald, Anne G. "Women on the Verge of a Glass-Ceiling Breakdown." Bioscience 61, no. 10 (October 2011): 823–825. doi:10.1525/bio.2011.61.10.12. https://doi.org/10.1525/bio.2011.61.10.12.

Russell, Aspen, and Heather Metcalf. "Transforming STEM Leadership Culture." Association for Women in Science, 2019. https://www.awis.org/leadership-report/.

Scheinert, Rachel. "The Science of Mentoring Women in Science—Judith Walters: Mentor Extraordinaire." The NIH Catalyst 23, no. 2 (March–April 2015). https://irp.nih.gov/catalyst/v23i2/the-science-of-mentoring-women-in-science.

Sharma, Shweta. "Our Work mostly Goes Unrecognized, Say Women Researchers (Science Feature)." Business Standard, February 9, 2014. https://www.business-standard.com/article/news-ians/our-work-mostly-goes-unrecognized-say-women-researchers-science-feature-114020900292_1.html.

Statista. "Percentage of the U.S. Population Who have Completed Four Years of College Or More from 1940 to 2020, by Gender." Last modified April 2021. https://www.statista.com/statistics/184272/educational-attainment-of-college-diploma-or-higher-by-gender/.

Tavernise, Sabrina, Claire Cain Miller, Quoctrung Bui, and Robert Gebeloff. "Why American Women Everywhere are Delaying Motherhood." The New York Times, June 16, 2021. https://www.nytimes.com/2021/06/16/us/declining-birthrate-motherhood.html.

U. S. Equal Employment Opportunity Commission. "Pregnancy Discrimination." Accessed February 11, 2022. https://www.eeoc.gov/pregnancy-discrimination#:~:text=The%20Pregnancy%20Discrimination%20Act%20(PDA,term%20or%20condition%20of%20employment.

Williams, Joan C. "The Maternal Wall." Harvard Business Review, October 2004. https://hbr.org/2004/10/the-maternal-wall.

CHAPTER 10: SEX PLUS AGE AND WISDOM

Abel, Amy Lui, and Diane Lim. "Why Retaining Older Women in the Workforce Will Help the U.S. Economy." Knowledge@Wharton, June 6, 2018. https://knowledge.wharton.upenn.edu/article/retaining-older-women-workforce-will-help-u-s-economy/.

Accenture. "Company Culture is Key to Unlocking Gender Equality and Narrowing Pay Gap, New Accenture Research Finds." Indonesian Newsroom, March 23, 2018. https://www.accenture.com/id-en/company-news-release-culture-unlocking-gender-equality.

Barnes, Patricia. "Age Discrimination is A Women's Issue that Women's Groups Tend to Ignore." Forbes, July 4, 2019. https://www.forbes.com/sites/patriciagbarnes/2019/07/04/age-discrimination-is-a-womens-issue-that-womens-groups-tend-to-ignore/?sh=ac9fa775dc76.

Bersin, Josh, and Tomas Chamorro-Premuzic. "The Case for Hiring Older Workers." Harvard Business Review, September 26, 2019. https://hbr.org/2019/09/the-case-for-hiring-older-workers.

Canning, Jessica, Maryam Haque, and Yimeng Wang. "Women at the wheel—Do Female Executives Drive Start-Up Success?" Dow Jones. 2012.

Diller, Vivian. "What are You really Feeling about Menopause, and how can You Talk about it?" Undated. https://www.poise. com/en-us/advice-and-support/expert-advice/article/lets-talk-what-are-you-really-feeling-about-menopause-and-how-can-you-talk-about-it.

Grose, Jessica. "Why is Perimenopause Still such a Mystery?" The New York Times, April 30, 2021. https://www.nytimes. com/2021/04/29/well/perimenopause-women.html?.?mc=aud_dev&ad-keywords=auddevgate&gclid=CjwKCAjwtfqKBhBoE-iwAZuesiMPmEBepCG7ILzog2xfYnQzO9qqdW72Lb3VP6r-ViCG7W2rs5IcbgkBoCdJ4QAvD_BwE&gclsrc=aw.ds.

Hardy, Claire, Eleanor Thorne, Amanda Griffiths, and Myra S. Hunter. "Work Outcomes in Midlife Women: The Impact of Menopause, Work Stress, and Working Environment." Women's Midlife Health 4, no. 1 (April 2018): 3. doi:10.1186/s40695-018-0036-z. https://doi.org/10.1186/s40695-018-0036-z.

HR Cloud. "The Age Diversity in the Workplace: How does it Impact Results?" Last modified August 13, 2021. https://www.hr-cloud.com/blog/the-age-diversity-in-the-workplace-how-does-it-impact-results#.

Ledford, Heidi. "Final Gender Discrimination Case at Salk Institute Ends in Settlement." Nature, November 22, 2018. https://www.nature.com/articles/d41586-018-07508-5.

Miller, Lisa. "Why We Need Older Women in the Workplace." The Cut, August 4, 2015. https://www.thecut.com/2015/08/why-we-need-older-women-in-the-workplace.html.

National Science Board. 2018 Science & Engineering Indicators. 2018.

Neumark, David, Ian Burn, and Patrick Button. "Is it Harder for Older Workers to Find Jobs? New and Improved Evidence from a Field Experiment." National Bureau of Economic Research. 2017.

Patterson, Jeneva. "It's Time to Start Talking About Menopause at Work." Harvard Business Review, February 24, 2020. https://hbr.org/2020/02/its-time-to-start-talking-about-menopause-at-work.

Pickett, Mallory. "'I Want what My Male Colleague has and that Will Cost a Few Million Dollars.'" New York Times Magazine, April 18, 2019. https://www.nytimes.com/2019/04/18/magazine/salk-institute-discrimination-science.html.

Place, Alyssa. "Yet another Hurdle for Women at Work: Their Age." Employee Benefit News, February 24, 2021. https://www.benefitnews.com/news/age-is-another-hurdle-for-women-at-work.

Rosenwald, Anne G. "Women on the Verge of a Glass-Ceiling Breakdown." Bioscience 61, no. 10 (October 2011): 823–825. doi:10.1525/bio.2011.61.10.12. https://doi.org/10.1525/bio.2011.61.10.12.

Saba, Katie, and Jacob Diker. "5 Benefits of Age Diversity in the Workplace." Circa, July 20, 2021. https://www.jdsupra.com/legalnews/5-benefits-of-age-diversity-in-the-9504111/#:~:text=Companies%20should%20continually%20look%20to,energy%20and%20eagerness%20to%20learn.

Scott, John. "In Early Results, COVID-19 Appears to have Little Impact on Retirement Preparation and Withdrawals." The Pew Charitable Trusts, May 26, 2021. https://www.pewtrusts.org/

en/research-and-analysis/issue-briefs/2021/05/in-early-results-covid-19-appears-to-have-little-impact-on-retirement-preparation-and-withdrawals.

Smith, Lindsey. "Top Female Scientists Cite 'Elite Boy's Club' as Reason Behind Discrimination Lawsuits at the Salk Institute." New York Minute, May 3, 2019. https://www.newyorkminutemag.com/salk-institute-faces-discrimination-lawsuits/.

Stevenson, Jane, and Dan Kaplan. "Women C-Suite Ranks Nudge Up—a Tad." Korn Ferry2019. https://www.kornferry.com/insights/this-week-in-leadership/women-in-leadership-2019-statistics.

Thomas, Rachel, Marianne Cooper, Kate McShane Urban, Gina Cardazone, Ali Bohrer, Sonia Mahajan, Lareina Yea, et al. Women in the workplace—2021. McKinsey & Company. 2021.

Wadman, Meredith. "Where are the Women?" Science, April 2, 2020. https://www.science.org/content/article/female-scientists-allege-discrimination-neglect-research-women-nih-s-child-health.

CHAPTER 11: HITTING THE WALL

Accenture. "Company Culture is Key to Unlocking Gender Equality and Narrowing Pay Gap, New Accenture Research Finds." Indonesian Newsroom, March 23, 2018. https://www.accenture.com/id-en/company-news-release-culture-unlocking-gender-equality.

Ammerman, Colleen, and Boris Groysberg. "Why the Crisis is Putting Companies at Risk of Losing Female Talent." Harvard Business Review, May 5, 2020. https://hbr.org/2020/05/why-the-crisis-is-putting-companies-at-risk-of-losing-female-talent.

Antecol, Heather, Kelly Bedard, and Jenna Stearns. "Equal but Inequitable: Who Benefits from Gender-Neutral Tenure Clock Stopping Policies?" American Economic Review 1008, no. 9 2018): 2420—2441. https://www.econstor.eu/bitstream/10419/142343/1/dp9904.pdf.

Bell, Michelle L., and Kelvin C. Fong. "Gender Differences in First and Corresponding Authorship in Public Health Research Submissions during the COVID-19 Pandemic." American Journal of Public Health 111, no. 1 (December 2020): 159–163. doi:10.2105/AJPH.2020.305975. https://doi.org/10.2105/AJPH.2020.305975.

Bendix, Aria. "Top WHO Official Laments Abuse, Death Threats Against Scientists: 'Being a Younger Female, I'm an Easy Target'." Insider, February 18, 2022. https://www.businessinsider.com/who-maria-van-kerkhove-abuse-death-threats-young-female-scientist-2022-2.

Cassella, Megan. "The Pandemic Drove Women Out of the Workforce. Will they Come Back?" Politico, July 7, 2021. https://www.politico.com/news/2021/07/22/coronavirus-pandemic-women-workforce-500329.

Deloitte. "Why Women are Leaving the Workforce After the Pandemic—And how to Win them Back." Forbes, July 1, 2021. https://www.forbes.com/sites/deloitte/2021/07/01/why-women-are-leaving-the-workforce-after-the-pandemic-and-how-to-win-them-back/?sh=3551d860796e.

Elflein, John. "COVID-19 Deaths Reported in the U.S. as of February 16, 2022, by Age." Last modified February 21, 2022. https://www.statista.com/statistics/1191568/reported-deaths-from-covid-by-age-us/.

Foster, Sarah. "Survey: 55% of Americans Expect to Search for a New Job Over the Next 12 Months." Bankrate, August 23, 2021. https://www.bankrate.com/personal-finance/job-seekers-survey-august-2021/.

Gogoi, Pallavi. "Stuck-at-Home Moms: The Pandemic's Devastating Toll on Women." NHPR, October 28, 2020. https://www.npr.org/2020/10/28/928253674/stuck-at-home-moms-the-pandemics-devastating-toll-on-women.

Gold, Jessica. "The Stress of being A Young, Female Scientific Expert during Covid-19." Forbes, November 24, 2020. https://www.forbes.com/sites/jessicagold/2020/11/24/the-stress-of-being-a-young-female-scientific-expert-during-covid-19/?sh=43b970875d66.

Gould, Elise. "Older Workers were Devastated by the Pandemic Downturn and Continue to Face Adverse Employment Outcomes." EPI testimony for the Senate Special Committee on Aging. Economic Policy Institute. April 29, 2021. https://www.epi.org/publication/older-workers-were-devastated-by-the-pandemic-downturn-and-continue-to-face-adverse-employment-outcomes-epi-testimony-for-the-senate-special-committee-on-aging/.

Hughes, Bryce E. "Coming Out in STEM: Factors Affecting Retention of Sexual Minority STEM Students." Science Advances 4, no. 3 (March 2018): eaao6373. https://doi.org/10.1126/sciadv.aao6373.

Jackson, Jon. "Fired Vaccination Chief Sues Tennessee Health Officials for Defamation." Newsweek, September 3, 2021. https://www.newsweek.com/fired-vaccination-chief-sues-tennessee-health-officials-defamation-1625893.

Kupec, Ivy. "COVID-19's Indirect Attack on Women." EMBL, August 26, 2020. https://www.embl.org/news/events/covid-19-indirect-attack-on-women/.

Mandavilli, Apoorva. "Could the Pandemic Prompt an 'Epidemic of Loss' of Women in the Sciences?" New York Times, April 20, 2021. https://www.nytimes.com/2021/04/13/health/women-stem-pandemic.html.

Mothers in Science. "Impact of COVID-19 Pandemic on Women in STEM." 2019. https://www.mothersinscience.com/covid19-resource.

Movement Advancement Project. "The Disproportionate Impacts of COVID-19 on LGBTQ Households in the U.S." Boulder, CO 2020. https://www.lgbtmap.org/file/2020-covid-lgbtq-households-report.pdf

Myers, Kyle R., Wei Yang Tham, Yian Yin, Nina Cohodes, Jerry G. Thursby, Marie C. Thursby, Peter Schiffer, Joseph T. Walsh, Karim R. Lakhani, and Dashun Wang. "Unequal Effects of the COVID-19 Pandemic on Scientists." Nature Human Behaviour 4, no. 9 (July 2020): 880-883. doi:10.1038/s41562-020-0921-y. https://doi.org/10.1038/s41562-020-0921-y.

National Science Foundation. Table 9-7. Employed Scientists and Engineers, by Ethnicity, Race, Occupation, Highest Degree Level, and Sex: 2019. Women, Minorities, and Persons with Disabilities in Science and Engineering. Alexandria, VA, 2021.

Nogrady, Bianca. "'I Hope You Die': How the COVID Pandemic Unleashed Attacks on Scientists." Nature, October 13, 2021. https://www.nature.com/articles/d41586-021-02741-x.

Parmelee, Michele, and Emma Codd. Women @ Work — A Global Outlook. Deloitte. 2021.

Ribarovska, Alana K., Mark R. Hutchinson, Quentin J. Pittman, Carmine Pariante, and Sarah J. Spencer. "Gender Inequality in Publishing during the COVID-19 Pandemic." Brain, Behavior, and Immunity 91 (January 2021): 1–3. doi:10.1016/j. bbi.2020.11.022. https://pubmed.ncbi.nlm.nih.gov/33212208 https://www.ncbi.nlm.nih.gov/pmc/articles/PMC7670232/.

Smith, Morgan. "January Jobs Report shows 'troubling' Signs for Women's Economic Recovery Amid Omicron Surge." CNBC, February 4, 2022. https://www.cnbc.com/2022/02/04/january-jobs-report-shows-troubling-signs-for-womens-economic-recovery.html.

Staniscuaski, Fernanda, Livia Kmetzsch, Rossana C. Soletti, Fernanda Reichert, Eugenia Zandonà, Zelia M. C. Ludwig, Eliade F. Lima, et al. "Gender, Race and Parenthood Impact Academic Productivity during the COVID-19 Pandemic: From Survey to Action." Frontiers in Psychology 12 (May 2021): 663252. doi:10.3389/fpsyg.2021.663252. https://pubmed.ncbi.nlm.nih. gov/34054667 https://www.ncbi.nlm.nih.gov/pmc/articles/ PMC8153681/.

Swift, Hannah J., and Alison L. Chasteen. "Ageism in the Time of COVID-19." Group Processes & Intergroup Relations 24, no. 2 (February 2021): 246–252. doi:10.1177/1368430220983452. https:// doi.org/10.1177/1368430220983452.

Thompson, Alex. "Biden's Top Science Adviser Bullied and Demeaned Subordinates, According to White House Investigation." Politico, February 7, 2022a. https://www.politico.com/news/2022/02/07/ eric-lander-white-house-investigation-00006077.

Thompson, Alex. "Biden's Top Science Adviser, Eric Lander, Re-
signs Amid Reports of Bullying." Politico, February 7, 2022b.
https://www.politico.com/news/2022/02/07/eric-lander-re-
signs-00006545.

U.S. Bureau of Labor Statistics. "Labor Force Statistics from the Current Population Survey." 2022. https://data.bls.gov/PDQWeb/ln.

Wenzel, Joseph. "Judge Denies Dr. Michelle Fiscus Claim to Monetary
Damages." News 4 Nashville, January 19, 2022. https://www.wsmv.
com/news/judge-denies-dr-michelle-fiscus-claim-to-monetary-
damages/article_c043eab0-796c-11ec-a01c-cf074a25f640.html.

Wu, Joy. "Pandemic Magnifies Gender Inequities, Provides Opportunities for Long-Range Solutions in Academic Medicine."
Stanford, the Clayman Institute for Gender Research, July
19, 2021. https://gender.stanford.edu/news-publications/gen-
der-news/pandemic-magnifies-gender-inequities-provides-op-
portunities-long-range

CHAPTER 12: CALLING ALL HUMANITY

Boston University. "Changing the Climate: How Public Health, Cities, and the Media can Advance Climate Solutions." Last modified April 20, 2018. https://www.bu.edu/sph/conversations/un-
categorized/changing-the-climate-how-public-health-cities-
and-the-media-can-advance-climate-solutions/.

CHE. "Precautionary Principle: The Wingspread Statement." 2019.
https://www.healthandenvironment.org/environmental-health/
social-context/history/precautionary-principle-the-wing-
spread-statement.

Cho, Renee. "Why Climate Science Needs More Women Scientists." Lamont-Doherty Earth Observatory, February 11, 2022.

https://lamont.columbia.edu/news/why-climate-science-needs-more-women-scientists.

Collaborative on Health and the Environment. "Climate Change and Infectious Diseases: Vector-Borne Diseases and Valley Fever." Last modified December 5, 2019. https://www.healthandenvironment.org/webinars/96503.

Congressional Research Service. Regulating Contaminants Under the Safe Drinking Water Act (SDWA) R46652. 2022.

Erickson, Britt E. Director. "TSCA was Reformed 4 Years Ago. Is the US Chemical Law Living Up to Expectations?" (Podcast). June 17, 2020.

Fang, Carolyn Y., and Zachary A. K. Frosch. "Understanding and Addressing Cancer Care Costs in the United States." JAMA Network Open 4, no. 10 (February 2021): e2127964. https://doi.org/10.1001/jamanetworkopen.2021.27964.

Foote, Eunice Newton. "Circumstances Affecting the Heat of the Sun's Rays." American Journal of Science and Arts 22 (1856): 382–393.

Francis, Pope, and Naomi Oreskes. 2015. "Encyclical on Climate Change and Inequality—On Care for our Common Home." 1st ed. Brooklyn and London: Melville House.

Gladstone, Brooke. The Psychological Toll of Working as a Climate Scientist. WNYC Studios, 2019.

Grandjean, Philippe, Clara Amalie, Gade Timmermann, Marie Kruse, Flemming Nielsen, Pernille Just Vinholt, Lasse Boding, Carsten Heilmann, and Kåre Mølbak. "Severity of COVID-19 at Elevated Exposure to Perfluorinated Alkylates." PLoS One 15, no. 12 (December 2020). doi:https://doi.org/10.1371/

journal.pone.0244815. https://journals.plos.org/plosone/article?id=10.1371/journal.pone.0244815.

Griggs, Troy, Andrew W. Lehren, Nadja Popovich, Anjali Singhvi, and Hiroko Tabuchi. "More than 40 Sites Released Hazardous Pollutants because of Hurricane Harvey." New York Times, September 8, 2017. https://www.nytimes.com/interactive/2017/09/08/us/houston-hurricane-harvey-harzardous-chemicals.html.

Hayhoe, Katharine. "Katharine Hayhoe, Climate Scientist." Last modified, n.d. http://www.katharinehayhoe.com/biography/.

Hayhoe, Katharine. The Most Important Thing You Can Do to Fight Climate Change: Talk about It. TEDWomen 2018.

Helldén, Daniel, Camilla Andersson, Maria Nilsson, Kristie L. Ebi, Peter Friberg, and Tobias Alfvén. "Climate Change and Child Health: A Scoping Review and an Expanded Conceptual Framework." 5, no. 3 (March 2021): e614–e175. doi:http://doi.org/10.1016/s2542-5196(20)30274-6. https://www.thelancet.com/journals/lanplh/article/PIIS2542-5196(20)30274-6/fulltext.

Hiatt, Robert A., and Naomi Beyeler. "Cancer and Climate Change." The Lancet Oncology 21, no. 11 (November 2020): e519-e527. doi:10.1016/S1470-2045(20)30448-4. https://doi.org/10.1016/S1470-2045(20)30448-4.

Intergovernmental Panel on Climate Change. "AR6 Synthesis Report: Climate Change 2022." 2022. https://www.ipcc.ch/report/sixth-assessment-report-cycle/.

Jackson, Roland. "Eunice Foote, John Tyndall and a Question of Priority." Notes and Records 74 (February 13, 2019): 105–118.

doi:https://doi.org/10.1098/rsnr.2018.0066. https://royalsoci-etypublishing.org/doi/10.1098/rsnr.2018.0066.

Jeffs, Nina. "Why Women's Leadership is Key to Climate Action." China Dialogue, January 18, 2022. https://chinadialogue.net/en/climate/why-womens-leadership-is-key-to-climate-action/.

Lu, Donna, and Lisa Cox. "Extreme Temperatures Kill 5 Million People a Year with Heat-Related Deaths Rising, Study Finds." The Guardian, July 7, 2021. https://www.theguardian.com/world/2021/jul/08/extreme-temperatures-kill-5-million-people-a-year-with-heat-related-deaths-rising-study-finds.

Park, Joohyun, and Kevin A. Look. "Health Care Expenditure Burden of Cancer Care in the United States." Inquiry: A Journal of Medical Care Organization, Provision and Financing 56 (January 2019): 46958019880696. doi:10.1177/0046958019880696. https://pubmed.ncbi.nlm.nih.gov/31583928 https://www.ncbi.nlm.nih.gov/pmc/articles/PMC6778988/.

Scottish Government and UN Women at COP26. "Gender Equality and Climate Change: Glasgow Women's Leadership Statement." Environment and Climate Change, Equality and Rights, November 2, 2021. https://www.gov.scot/publications/glasgow-womens-leadership-statement-gender-equality-climate-change/.

Sea Level Rise.org. "America's Sea Level has Risen by 6.5 Inches since 1950." Last modified, n.d. https://sealevelrise.org.

Shabir, Osman. "The Effect of Climate Change on Asthma." News Medical Life Sciences, January 17, 2022. https://www.news-medical.net/health/The-Effect-of-Climate-Change-on-Asthma.aspx.

Steffen, Will, Johan Rockström, Katherine Richardson, Timothy M. Lenton, Carl Folke, Diana Liverman, Colin P. Summerhayes, et al. "Trajectories of the Earth System in the Anthropocene." Proceedings of the National Academy of Sciences USA 115, no. 33 (August 2018): 8252. doi:10.1073/pnas.1810141115. http://www.pnas.org/content/115/33/8252.abstract.

Tamman, Maurice. "Men Dominate Climate Science. She Made It to the Top—and Did It Her Own Way." Reuters, April 21, 2021a. https://www.reuters.com/investigates/special-report/climate-change-scientists-lequere/.

Tamman, Maurice. "The Reuters Hot List." Reuters, April 20, 2021b. https://www.reuters.com/investigates/special-report/climate-change-scientists-list/.

U.N. Climate Change News. "Overrepresentation of Men in UN Climate Process Persists." UN Climate Change News, October 1, 2021. https://unfccc.int/news/overrepresentation-of-men-in-un-climate-process-persists.

U.N. "What is Climate Change?" Last modified, n.d. https://www.un.org/en/climatechange/what-is-climate-change.

U.S. Department of Health and Human Services. "Cancer and the Environment: What you need to know what you can do." National Institute of Environmental Health Services, National Cancer Institute, and National Institute of Environmental Health Services, August 2003. https://www.niehs.nih.gov/health/materials/cancer_and_the_environment_508.pdf.

U.S. Department of Health and Human Services. "HHS Unveils Climate Adaptation and Resilience Plan and Policy Statement." Last modified October 7, 2021. https://www.hhs.gov/about/news/2021/10/07/hhs-unveils-climate-adaptation-and-resilience-plan-and-policy-statement.html.

U.S. Environmental Protection Agency. "Our Mission and what we Do." Last modified July 2, 2021. https://www.epa.gov/aboute-pa/our-mission-and-what-we-do.

U.S. Environmental Protection Agency. "Statistics for the New Chemicals Review Program Under TSCA." Last modified January 3, 2022. https://www.epa.gov/reviewing-new-chemicals-un-der-toxic-substances-control-act-tsca/statistics-new-chemi-cals-review#stats.

USGCRP. The Impacts of Climate Change on Human Health in the United States: A Scientific Assessment. Washington, DC, 2016.

Watts, Nick, Markus Amann, Nigel Arnell, Sonja Ayeb-Karlsson, Kristine Belesova, Maxwell Boykoff, Peter Byass, et al. "The 2019 Report of the Lancet Countdown on Health and Climate Change: Ensuring that the Health of a Child Born Today is Not Defined by a Changing Climate." The Lancet 394, no. 10211 (November 2019): 1836–1878. doi:https://doi.org/10.1016/S0140-6736(19)32596-6. https://www.sciencedirect.com/science/arti-cle/pii/S0140673619325966.

White House, The. "Executive Order on Tackling the Climate Cri-sis at Home and Abroad." January 27, 2021. https://www.white-house.gov/briefing-room/presidential-actions/2021/01/27/execu-tive-order-on-tackling-the-climate-crisis-at-home-and-abroad/.

CHAPTER 13: WE CAN DO THIS!

Alter, Charlotte, Suyin Haynes, and Justin Worland. "2019 Person of the Year—Greta Thunberg." Time Magazine2019. https://time.com/person-of-the-year-2019-greta-thunberg/.

Ayotte, Joseph D., Laura Medalie, Sharon L. Qi, Lorraine C. Backer, and Bernard T. Nolan. "Estimating the High-Arsenic Domestic-Well Population in the Conterminous United States." Environmental Science & Technology 51, no. 21 (November 2017): 12443–12454. doi:10.1021/acs.est.7b02881. https://doi.org/10.1021/acs.est.7b02881.

Chakradhar, Shraddha. "New Pediatrician Network Puts Spotlight on Climate Change's Effects on Children." Stat, December 18, 2020. https://www.statnews.com/2020/12/18/new-pediatrician-network-puts-spotlight-on-climate-changes-effects-on-children/.

Dash, Mike. "Aqua Tofana: Slow-Poisoning and Husband-Killing in 17th Century Italy." Mike Dash History, April 6, 2015. https://mikedashhistory.com/2015/04/06/aqua-tofana-slow-poisoning-and-husband-killing-in-17th-century-italy/.

Davis, Pamela B., Emma A. Meagher, Claire Pomeroy, William L. Lowe, Arthur H. Rubenstein, Joy Y. Wu, Anne B. Curtis, and Rebecca D. Jackson. "Pandemic-Related Barriers to the Success of Women in Research: A Framework for Action." Nature Medicine (February 2022). doi:10.1038/s41591-022-01692-8. https://doi.org/10.1038/s41591-022-01692-8.

DHHS News. "NH's High Bladder Cancer Rate Prompts State to Urge Testing Private Wells for Arsenic." In-Depth NH, May 9, 2018. http://indepthnh.org/2018/05/09/nhs-high-bladder-cancer-rate-prompts-state-to-urge-testing-private-wells-for-arsenic/.

Francis, Pope, and Naomi Oreskes. 2015. Encyclical on Climate Change and Inequality — On Care for our Common Home. First ed. Brooklyn and London: Melville House.

Laville, Sandra. "Air Pollution a Cause in Girl's Death, Coroner Rules in Landmark Case." The Guardian, December 16, 2020.

https://www.theguardian.com/environment/2020/dec/16/girls-death-contributed-to-by-air-pollution-coroner-rules-in-land-mark-case.

Marks, Elizabeth, Caroline Hickman, Panu Pihkala, Susan Clay-ton, Eric R. Lewandowski, Elouise E. Mayall, Britt Wray, Ca-triona Mellor, and Lise van Susteren. "Young People's Voices on Climate Anxiety, Government Betrayal and Moral Injury: A Global Phenomenon." SSRN, September 7, 2021. doi:http://dx.doi.org/10.2139/ssrn.3918955. https://ssrn.com/abstract=3918955.

Messmer, Mindi, McConnell, Jim, Cushing, Renny, Grassie, Chuck, Altschiller, Deb, and Fraser, Karen. HB 1592—An Act Requir-ing the Commissioner of the Department of Environmental Services to Review Ambient Groundwater Standards for Ar-senic.2017.

Pruitt-Young, Sharon. "Young People are Anxious about Climate Change and Say Governments are Failing Them." NPR, Sep-tember 14, 2021. https://www.npr.org/2021/09/14/1037023551/climate-change-children-young-adults-anxious-worried-study.

Scottish Government and UN Women at COP26. "Gender Equal-ity and Climate Change: Glasgow Women's Leadership State-ment." Environment and Climate Change, Equality and Rights, November 2, 2021. https://www.gov.scot/publications/glasgow-womens-leadership-statement-gender-equality-cli-mate-change/.

Smith, Roger. "Arsenic: A Murderous History—The King of Poi-sons." Dartmouth Toxic Metals Superfund Research Program, n.d., n.d. https://sites.dartmouth.edu/toxmetal/arsenic/arse-nic-a-murderous-history/.

University of Pittsburgh and United Nations Development Programme. Global Report on Gender Equality in Public Administration. 2021.

Whorton, James C. 2010. "The Arsenic Century: How Victorian Britain was Poisoned at Home, Work and Play." Oxford and New York: Oxford University Press.

RESOURCES

Female disruptors database: https://bit.ly/femalescientist

NH Science and Public Health, Science for Public Good: https://www.nhscience.org

Association for Women in Science, Celebrating Pioneering Women in Science: https://www.awis.org/historical-women-scientists/

Dartmouth Toxic Metals | Superfund Research Program: https://sites.dartmouth.edu/toxmetal/

Environmental Working Group, resources about chemicals: https://www.ewg.org

LessCancer, National Cancer Prevention Workshops: https://www.youtube.com/channel/UCl7MB10j29spCIKmCjQoLvQ

Retraction Watch, Tracking retractions as a window into the scientific process: https://retractionwatch.com

Scientific Integrity Digest, A blog about science integrity, by Elisabeth Bik: https://scienceintegritydigest.com

U.S. Environmental Protection Agency, PFAS Master List of PFAS Substances: https://comptox.epa.gov/dashboard/chemical-lists/pfasmaster

We Are Teachers website, "16 Wonderful Women Scientists to Inspire Your Students:" https://www.weareteachers.com/women-scientists/